FELSTED PREPARATORY SCHOOL
THE FIRST HUNDRED YEARS
1895–1995

FELSTED
PREPARATORY
SCHOOL
THE FIRST 100 YEARS
1895-1995

D. J. ARMOUR

ATHLONE
London & Atlantic Highlands, N.J.

First published 1995 by
THE ATHLONE PRESS LTD
1 Park Drive, London NW11 7SG
and 165 First Avenue,
Atlantic Highlands, NJ 07716

British Library Cataloguing in Publication Data
A catalogue record for this book is available
from the British Library

ISBN 0 485 11482 8

Library of Congress Cataloging-in-Publication Data
Armour, D. J., 1933–
  Felsted Preparatory School : the first 100 years, 1895–1995
/ D. J. Armour.
    p. cm.
  Includes index.
  ISBN 0-485-11482-8
  1. Felsted Preparatory School--History   I. Title.
LF795.F4A76   1995
373.43--dc20   95-6401
                                                        CIP

Typeset by
Bibloset

Printed and bound in Great Britain by
the University Press, Cambridge

Contents

Preface   vii
Acknowledgements   ix

1   Early Days 1892–1907   1
2   Frederick Jacob 1907–1933   9
3   Andrew C Telfer 1933–1946   27
4   B S Morris 1946–1951   37
5   The Rev D L Ross 1951–1971   45
6   O J B Pemberton 1971–1978   57
7   T M Andrews 1978–1991   67
8   M P Pomphrey 1992–   77

Appendix 1: F. Jacob, Esq.   81
Appendix 2: The Prep. Thirty Years Ago   83
Appendix 3: The Origin of our League Names   87
Appendix 4: Assistant Staff at the Preparatory School
            from 1920   91
Appendix 5: Names   95
Index   97

Preface

At least one previous Headmaster of Felsted Preparatory School put forward a plan for extending the age range of the pupils that the school could educate, but at the time the governing body of the School were not receptive to that particular idea. Then in 1992, partly through economic necessity, that body received and extended the plan to embrace both a pre-preparatory department and co-education at the same time. Up to that point the Preparatory School had been very much a conventional boys' boarding school and, although old habits and routines (and memories) take time to fade, it seemed most appropriate, indeed important, that someone should record what had gone on in the School since its birth in 1895.

Donald Armour, in a typically modest way, agreed that he was well-placed – and interested enough – to carry out the task. As any reader of this record will see, Donald has been tireless in this efforts to search the dusty corners of the School's past. In so doing he will recall to the minds of many former pupils (and Staff) who study this history the events and faces that early schooling, but particularly that in a prep. school, indelibly print in a young boy's memory.

I congratulate Donald on what he has produced and alongside others, particularly those who have preceded me, thank him for all his efforts.

Michael Pomphrey
Felsted, 1995

Acknowledgements

As will be appreciated, a wide variety of sources has been used in compiling this account. Material for the years up to 1933 was particularly sparse, and I am grateful to Mr M R Craze for his permission to draw on the relevant pages in his 'History of Felsted School'. He also read through the script and made many valuable suggestions. I was fortunate in having the recollections of Mr K B Turner who was at the Prep. before World War I and was thus present during the early days of the Jacob era. Mr H E Walker was able to provide a rich fund of detail on the way in which Jacob ran the school in the 1920s, and Mr C O Marriner was able to give further information concerning this time.

For the war-time evacuation to Herefordshire I have referred to 'Felsted in Herefordshire', to the occasional Junior House magazines of the time and to conversations with Mrs Telfer who also kindly checked the script. Mr B S Morris provided much significant information about his five years as Headmaster, and Mr G S Jameson was able to span this period and the earlier years of the Rev D L Ross's headmastership with much welcome detail.

As was to be expected, the last two or three decades are provided with an embarrassing quantity of information both from the 'Young Felstedian' and from the memories of those who took part. Mrs M Ronaldson gave much help in conversation and by lending me her papers relating to the 1964 'A Felsted Chronicle'. Mrs D L Ross was kind enough to read the section recounting the years during which she and her husband Derek were at Felsted, and Miss B Tozer and Mr J T Packett cast a critical eye over the passages of which they had personal knowledge.

My thanks are also due to Mr N S Hinde for affording me free access to the Felsted School Archives and for lending photographs for the illustrations.

The long task of putting the typescript and frequent revisions on to disc was willingly undertaken by Mrs S C Whitear and Miss Susannah Pomphrey, to whom I am most grateful.

D.J.A.

1

Early Days 1892–1907

The end of the Nineteenth Century witnessed a remarkable growth in the size and wealth of the middle classes in Britain, which was reflected in the dramatic increase in the number of preparatory schools. These schools, almost exclusively for boys up to the age of 13, were nearly all owned by their headmasters. A number of these headmasters gathered in March 1892, originally to determine the size and weight of cricket balls to be used in prep school matches. In December of that year a further conference met to discuss more serious academic matters, a committee was elected, and this committee founded the Association of Headmasters of Preparatory Schools. In 1923 the AHPS became the IAPS, the Incorporated Association of Preparatory Schools.

Into this general context we may place the proposal in the same year, 1892, by Felsted Headmaster H A Dalton to start a separate Preparatory House for the boys at Felsted under 13. Was Dalton moved by recent events in the prep school world, or did he simply wish to make available extra accommodation for the older boys in the main school? It could well have been the latter. At Speech Day in 1894 Dalton's report included these words,

> The Headmaster then turned to the various changes that had lately been made. The past year had brought Mr Miller to Felsted, and his Preparatory School, so nearly completed, would at once enable the space to be used for other purposes, and give parents an opportunity of ensuring an education under proper

supervision for their sons until they are old enough to enter a public school.

In September 1893 Mr and Mrs C M Miller came to Felsted from St Peter's School, York. They built their preparatory school at their own expense on one of the fields which the Governors had bought at the sale of Garnett's Farm in July 1893, giving the Governors the option of purchase at a possible later date. The building work was done by Mr Brown of Braintree.

At the beginning of 1894 the foundations were laid in a garden which had belonged to a Mr Smith. His wife was known as 'Mrs Smoggs' and used to sell sweets in the village. In the front garden of the new building stood a saddlery shop which belonged to Mr George Wright. He moved to a house in the Chelmsford Road opposite Felsted Place. While their school was being built, the Millers lived at Priory Lodge on the Dunmow Road facing the railway station.

An Opening Service was conducted by the Bishop of St Albans on November 29th 1894, and in the following January the Preparatory House started with 39 boys, full capacity being 50. At Speech Day of that year the Headmaster said that,

> The numbers had risen to 250, an increase which had been made possible by the successful establishment, under the happiest auspices, of the Preparatory School. This was nearly full. He had every confidence in its future success, and felt that thanks were due to Mr Miller for his enterprise in building the House.

Most of the boys came from Backhouse's, part of 'Big School', a separate boarding house built by the Rev J H Backhouse, Second Master 1851 to 1870, in Headmaster Grignon's time. In the Victorian School House the Trustees built first a Second Master's House and next a Headmaster's House. Backhouse lived in this from 1861 – 70 and it kept his name. In 1890 boys under 13 had been segregated from the rest and put there in charge of the Music Master and a Resident Assistant Matron. Now moved to Miller's new Preparatory House, they were in two Forms known as Divisions, taught by Miller himself and two other masters, Mr L G Duckworth and Mr J W D Thorp (O.F.). The Felstedian of January 1895 noted,

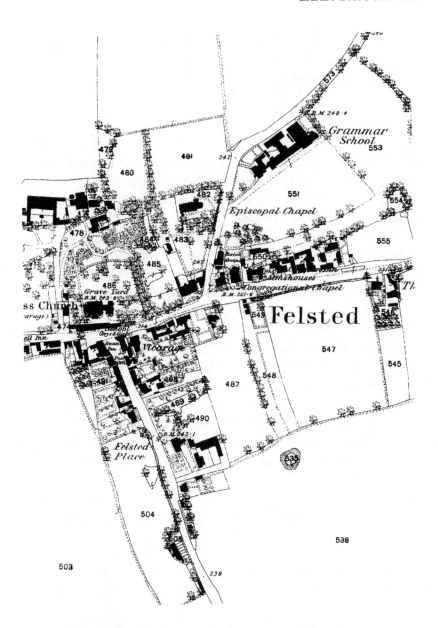

Figure 1: From the Ordnance Survey map of 1875 showing the original purchase of land (487, 548, 549) and land acquired for playing fields in 1923 (545, 547). Follyfield House was built on part of this land in 1929. Reproduced by courtesy of the Essex Record Office.

> . . . the Preparatory School, which is now in full swing with the substantial number of thirty nine boys. Several of these have been removed from 'Backhouse's', which ancient institution, alas!, is now, strictly speaking, dead, and its former inhabitants will no doubt be missed, if by the Prefects alone, to whom they were, to say the least of it, most necessary.

Yet at the end of the Summer Term 1896 the Millers left. Their reasons for leaving so soon after starting what appeared to be a successful venture can only be guessed. They stayed in Essex, going to Copford, near Colchester, where they started a private school. The Preparatory House they had built at Felsted was leased to the Governors until 1910.

The Rev A V Grégoire was appointed Head. The school was at full capacity with 50 boys, and a third Assistant Master was taken on. Until 1907, when Jacob came, the boys were lodged and fed there but were taught in 'Big School'. Rev Grégoire stayed until 1903. He was a bachelor who drove the boys hard and unsympathetically, and numbers had fallen to 24. He left to start his own school in Bath, taking some of the Felsted boys with him.

Dr F Stephenson, the School's Medical Officer, took over from him. At the same time the school's name changed from the Preparatory House to the Junior House, by which it was called until 1956. At the age of 35, without having completed a full term as Head, Dr Stephenson died on the 21st March 1904 of pneumonia. His wife remained in charge for the rest of the school year, until she was succeeded by the new Medical Officer, Dr W S Frith.

To give a flavour of those far off Edwardian days, the following items have been gleaned from the 1st Volume of the Felsted Preparatory House Magazine.

> *December 1898.* And now a few words as to our games. For the first two football seasons we played football on our own field adjoining to the House, where we also play cricket. Of course it was very nice to have a football ground so near, but as we played almost up to the end of the Lent Term, the turf had not much chance of recovering itself for the cricket next term. The result was that the pitches were simply awful, and during the Summer Term of 1898 we played cricket on a cocoa-nut (sic) matting pitch, and the following winter the middle of the field was entirely relaid

with turf from Easton Lodge, so that last term we got some very fair wickets.

Meanwhile our football had a chequered career. At first we went over to Big School and played on a ground close to the Swimming Pool [opened for use 23rd November 1895]. This was not a success, and last Winter Term we had a ground on the Stebbing Road, close to the railway bridge, and this term we have moved again to one of the Bury Fields on the way to the Station.

In the Summer Term we play matches against Junior House Rooms and Forms from the School, and in addition to this we went over to Cambridge to play against the King's College Choir Boys, on whom we hope to have our revenge next year. One Summer Term, three years ago, we journeyed to Bishops Stortford to play against a Preparatory School there, and we gave them a good thrashing; but as there were only eleven boys in the school, we must not be too conceited. This match has been given up!

The use of turf from Easton Lodge is interesting. Frances 'Daisy' Maynard, Countess of Warwick, from 1893, replaced Lily Langtree in the Prince of Wales's affections, until she in turn gave way to Alice Keppel. Her husband, the Earl of Warwick, had been a Governor of Felsted School since 1894, and a report of Speech Day 1897 shows a strong connection between Easton Lodge and Felsted.

For pleasant weather, crowded grounds, bright apparel and a successfully executed programme, Speech Day this year equalled if not surpassed all preceding occasions. We have never seen the Big Schoolroom so full before nor so bright with flowers and dresses. We were disappointed at the absence of the Earl of Warwick, although the Headmaster remarked that the speeches would be shortened by one. The Countess of Warwick drove over in the afternoon. We cannot let the opportunity slip of thanking them both for their kind invitation to the School generally to visit Easton Lodge on the last day of term.

At this time there was a School cricket fixture with a local team at Easton Lodge, so that it would indeed be a likely source of turf for the new Preparatory House's playing field.

On the 31st May 1899 the first Fathers' Match was played. The boys won by 17 runs. It has been an annual fixture ever since.

The Cricket XI report for 1900 shows a master-in-charge clearly disillusioned by his team. After noting that the 1st XI Played 8, Won

5, Lost 2, Drawn 1, he writes sourly, 'As usual, the Captain has lost the bowling analysis ...', and goes on to list the Cricket Characters in less than flattering terms.

> * *H M Hankin* (Captain). Most disappointing as a bat; is entirely lacking in vigour, and rarely makes runs. A fair change bowler.
> * *H W Partridge*. Most disappointing, after his promise of last year. Generally retires after the first straight ball. A fair field and a poor bowler.
> * *C N Peel*. The best bat in the eleven, but never came off in matches. Good field at cover and a fair change bowler.
> * *K E Kinder*. A poor bat who thinks that discretion is the better part of valour. Retires first to square leg and then to the tent, whenever a straight ball is bowled at him. A good field.
> * *E S Ulyat*. A good, painstaking bat who has come on a great deal. Is practically at the top of the averages. A good field and a fairly safe catch.
> * *L D Sweetlove*. A good, medium pace bowler with a strong affection for the leg side. Has done some very good bowling performances. A merry bat who occasionally gets runs, but to no recognised rules.
> * *R W Marriage*. Shows promise of being a hard hitting bat. Did not play during the latter part of the term, through illness. Keeps wicket fairly well.
> *R C Lyle*. A painstaking bat with an apologetic style. Has got runs at critical times. His bat drives well. Slow in the field.
> *N H Prendergast*. An improving bat and is not afraid to play forward. Does not run very fast in the field.
> *A E L Muddiman*. A very fair little bowler. Misses catches occasionally.
> *W S Lyle*. A weak bat and a poor field – he takes the game very seriously.

> * Colour

A great interest at the turn of the century was egg collecting, actively encouraged by the masters. A cabinet, in the form of a triptych, capable of holding 176 bird's eggs, was put in the dining room. It was made by Mr Key, the school carpenter to a design by Mr Tregelles, one of the staff. He also drew up a list of eggs, 'all of which we eventually hope to possess'. The target list given to boys numbered 138 species and included present rarities like the Dartford Warbler, Ring Ouzel and Merlin.

Mr Arthur Key died in 1923. He had resigned through ill health early in the Great War after 30 years' service as the school carpenter. 'Up to his death his very diminutive figure with white side whiskers and a remarkable clear complexion was frequently to be seen in Braintree.' The oak desk in the sanctuary in the chapel and, partially, the clock in the original Grignon Hall were also pieces of his work.

In 1899 the first separate Sunday services for the Preparatory House were held with Matins at 9.45 and Evensong at 5.15. Weekday services were still attended in company with the main school. At this time Anglican Chant superseded Gregorian Chant in chapel.

In 1900 the Preparatory House was wired for 'The ELECTRIC light'. The report in the Magazine read, 'the Electric Light just managed to put in its first appearance on the first afternoon of the first day of term. It has behaved very well so far, having only failed us once for about an hour'.

A change was made to the uniform in the same year which has lasted to the present day. 'The House blazer has been changed from the green of various shades of shabbiness to scarlet which will not fade. Scarlet stockings are also worn for football.'

Also in 1900 'Mr Elwyn's House opened across the road'.

Terms were similar to those of today, but the Summer Term was about three weeks longer than it is now. The dates for 1900 were,

Spring Term	Jan 19 to Apr 5	11 weeks
Summer Term	May 4 to Aug 1	13 weeks
Autumn Term	Sep 20 to Dec 21	13 weeks

The Boer War was fully reported in the FPH Magazine in a series of articles which were thoughtful, well balanced and devoid of the jingoism which they could so easily have expressed. Another interesting series described other Public Schools and was entitled 'About Other People'. Wellington, Rossall, Rugby, Winchester and Uppingham were the schools discussed, and there was a similar account of life 'at the Varsity'. The articles in the Magazine were meaty but far from stodgy.

Indeed, they contained much quiet humour and were informative and written carefully. They seem to anticipate from their schoolboy readers a higher standard of literacy than would be expected today.

The Felsted Preparatory House Magazine did not last long – from

1898 to 1901, 'Let us shed an appreciative tear', reminisced one OF, 'for, while it lived, it was a merry little paper'. A short lived series of a prep school magazine appeared from time to time from then until 1948 when the current 'Young Felstedian' made its first appearance.

In 1906 Rev Frank Stephenson was appointed Headmaster of Felsted School, when H A Dalton, after 15 years in office, moved to the Headmastership of Harrison College, Barbados as a health cure for his wife. Two years earlier J W D Thorp had gone there for his health and suggested Dalton's name to the electors of the College. The School as a whole was in debt, having borrowed money for the new Engineering and Carpentry Shops. The Junior House, averaging only 27 boys in the previous three years, was uneconomical. More income was needed to pay off the debt. As the Governors were reluctant to put up the fees, more pupils had to be attracted. Next year, 1907, Dr Frith's contract was terminated, and he returned to private practice. Stephenson appointed a former colleague from Cheltenham College to be Head of the Junior House. This man was Frederick Jacob.

2

Frederick Jacob
1907 – 1933

Jacob was 34 years old when he took up his appointment and had recently married. He had gone to school at Sandwich and started a career in accountancy. When he came of age, he gave this up and went to Caius College, Cambridge. Playing as a forward, he won Rugger Blues in 1895 and 1896, represented Blackheath and was capped eight times for England. After leaving Cambridge he taught at Bradfield and then at Cheltenham. At Cheltenham he met Frank Stephenson, and when they were both at Felsted, 'they formed an unbroken alliance. They ultimately left the school together in 1933'.

Not only was Jacob a great athlete, he was also a convinced Christian, and at Cambridge had been a Sunday School teacher with Puritan principles. He ruled the Junior House for the next 26 years on the lines of these principles.

The school was divided into the five Leagues which still exist – Cromwell, Gaselee, Grignon, Lord Riche and Smythies. (The origin of the League names are given in Appendix 3). At the end of each term the League with the most 'plus points' was presented with a silver challenge cup, representing St George slaying the Dragon, an appropriate symbol of the ethos which Jacob was trying to instil. Boys were rewarded with plus points and penalised with minus points, which could add up to vast totals every week. This system prevailed until the early 1970s when it was modified and then finally came to an end. The duties of League Captains were clearly defined and printed on a card, and show the moral tone which he was trying to establish from the start. It read:

DUTIES OF CAPTAINS
1 To see that each member actually does his particular job when the League is on duty.
2 To see that each boy in the dormitory, including himself, gets out of bed directly the bell rings and does not get back again, and that there is no talking after 'Lights'.
3 To squash promptly any kind of bullying.
4 To see that nothing goes wrong morally with the League, especially in the dormitory.
5 To ask himself, 'What is best for the League?', not 'What is best for me?' and not to use his power and influence for his own selfish advantage (fagging other fellows, for example).
6 To be keen and energetic, and to do his best to keep others up to the mark.
7 To be a 'real white man', that is to do nothing mangy, mean or under hand.
8 To do his duty, even at the risk of being unpopular.
9 Not to use physical force in the League under any circumstances.

League Captains usually applied for the position and could ask to lead a League other than the one in which they had originally started. They chose their own Vice-Captains. They bore a considerable amount of responsibility and sometimes lost points because of a misdemeanour on the part of someone else in their League. This was thought to be rather unjust, but Jacob considered that the offence should have been prevented by the Captain.

Every term four of the five Leagues drew up a duty roster for their League. The period of duty varied according to the position of the League in the points competition during the previous term. The top League was excused duties, while the others had periods in the ratio 4:3:2:1. Thus the bottom League spent nearly half the term doing odd jobs.

Occasional Junior House reports were printed in the Felstedian for a short time. That for Nov 1914, evidently written by Jacob, reads,

> The moral plane needs a lengthier treatment than the others. The standard of honour has been fairly high. It would be Utopian to expect that in a community of fifty four all would value equally the saying that honesty is the best policy. There have been occasional attempts to adopt the tactics of card-sharpers in the solution of difficulties, but public opinion has set its face against these un-English methods.
>
> The round-shouldered, hand-in-pockets sloucher has very nearly died out, but he dies hard, like the wireworm, and it would perhaps be truer to say that he has been scotched rather than been killed. There are some who say that the condition of round shoulders is a physical and not a moral weakness and others maintained that the earth is flat.

Jacob made an immediate and lasting impression on the boys in his charge. He expected them to strive for the athleticism which he had achieved and looked for excellence on the playing field, in the Gymnasium and in the Swimming Bath. Success for one's side was, in his eyes, more important than success for oneself. He introduced Rugger at the Junior House, and it subsequently replaced Association Football at the Senior School. There the first Rugger XV was assembled in the Autumn Term of 1917, and the first match was played against Haileybury 2nd XV on Saturday, November 10th. The team was taught the game and coached by Jacob who also refereed matches. (Felsted lost by 2 tries to 1 goal and 4 tries – 6-17).

Photographs of Jacob show an impeccably groomed man, and he expected the boys to follow his example. Bootlaces had to be tied in the 'Jacob' knot so that no loose ends could be seen. The school grounds received the same attention, and tradition had it that he never went to bed, for late at night and early morning he could be seen on hands and knees weeding the playing fields. He was also famous in the county for his expertise with a scythe, which extended to cutting rushes, a feat which had to be seen to be believed. On Thursday evening he practised bell-ringing in the Parish Church.

Good behaviour in the dining room was spelled out in his 'Hints on Table Manners', a copy of which was given to every boy. Most of the 'Hints' are relevant, if not practised today, but the concluding comment

11

on Self-mastery and Self-control is pure Jacob.

Hints on Table Manners
(Which we all know but are sometimes too lazy to practise)

1 Sit up straight with shoulders pressed back and down, and your elbows close to your sides in an easy natural position. This is one of the best methods for strengthening the muscles of the back.
2 Do not put your arms on the table, which is a privilege of age. If your plate is in the proper place and you are holding your knife and fork correctly, it will be quite unnecessary to touch the table with your sleeves.
3 Do not drink or speak while you have food in your mouth. It saves time undoubtedly, but that is not always a virtue.
4 Do not pick up a large slice of cake or bread and butter, and bite away at the end like a dog gnawing a bone. Use your knife and cut your food into pieces that can be handled easily.
5 Do not bite pieces off your bread at dinner, but break them off.
6 Do not grip your knife, fork, or spoon as if you intended to use them as oars in a rowing race. The end of the handles of the knife and fork should touch the palm at the root of the thumb; the back of the handle of the spoon (or of the fork used as a spoon) should rest against the forefinger on the side nearest the thumb.
7 Do not use your spoon alone, for puddings, etc, now that you have left the nursery. If you can manage with one implement only, take your fork.
8 Do not fidget with your knife, fork, spoon, or table-napkin ring, and fold up your table-napkin neatly before leaving the table.
9 Wipe your mouth after drinking and give it a final polish before leaving the table, especially after eating an egg. It is a duty you owe to your companions to avoid being personally repulsive.
10 Do not put your head down to your cup when drinking, but lift it to your mouth with your hand.
11 Do not blow your nose at meal-times unless it is absolutely necessary, and in that case, do it very quietly, not like a ploughboy.
12 Do not forget to say 'Please,' and 'Thank you,' to your companions and the servants.
13 Do not stretch in front of anyone, but ask him to pass you what you want.
14 Take your soup from the side of the spoon, not from the end, and do not make any noise while doing so.
15 Keep your lips closed while eating and do not 'smack' them.
16 Take the top slice, not the one you fancy most.
17 Put your hand before your mouth when you yawn, for no one would care to see the inside of it.
18 Remember that good manners are merely a part of efficiency, which

is another name for Self-mastery or Self-control.

FELSTED SCHOOL, ESSEX.

The section on the Junior House in the Felsted School prospectus of 1907 bears Jacob's unmistakable stamp. It ends with these words:

> Great stress is laid on good manners and tidiness, and though every possible precaution is taken to promote the health of the boys, they are not pampered in any way, and no efforts are spared to make them straight, manly and self-reliant – worthy citizens of a great Empire.
>
> The total inclusive fee is £81-1-0d per annum. The only extras are instrumental music, books and private lessons.

By concentrating so single-mindedly on instilling the knightly virtues, it is not surprising that academic learning occupied a secondary place at the Junior House. Few scholarships were awarded, and not many Junior House boys found their way into the Sixth Form at the Senior School.

In 1912, at the Southern end of Miller's original building an extension was built, gymnasium and classrooms below and Cromwell dormitory above. The boys were now taught on the premises, and the Junior House became a self-contained and economic unit with accommodation for 50 boys. In 1909 'a galvanised iron addition' was constructed as a temporary building, which lasted until 1970 – the 'gym' as it was known. It was finally removed to make way for the present Ross Hall.

I am indebted to Mr K B Turner, grandfather of Julian (fh 1979 – 88) and Timothy (fh 1981 – 90) Hamilton for these recollections of the Prep before the First World War. They mention most of the features of Jacob's system, and extracts from a later account in this section show how little had changed in the intervening years.

> K B Turner (Kenneth): I was born at Barnston Hall 5th June 1900. Taught at home by a governess. In 1910 entered the Prep as a day boy. Great War started Summer of 1914. Went over to Senior School, Felsted, September 1914 in Montgomery's House. Still a day boy until Sixth Form. In Summer 1918 failed to join Royal Flying Corps due to poor eyesight. Accepted as an Officer Cadet in the Royal Engineers.

Told to stay on at Felsted in OTC until called up for next Officer Course. Armistice November 11th – still no call up. I had meanwhile obtained a post-war entry into Caius College, Cambridge. I was thus told that I was free of Army call-up, and in January 1919 went up to Caius to read for the Engineering Tripos, a schoolboy among large numbers of serving Officers coming out of the Forces.

The Prep Buildings, etc.: Just the present main block with corrugated iron Playroom/Gym on the site of Ross Hall. An entry from the road with drive around to the left to the Master's front door and on to his stable block (present bootroom and HM's garage). The boys' entrance in similar position to present, but most of car park area (now the 'Quad') was then a garden to Lawsell's.

All the Follyfield area was farmland up to the road. The playing field (now Cloisterfield) was much as at present behind Lawsell's and the butcher's shop. (Telfer's classroom and dormitory wing was yet to be built – in 1934.)

Jacob: was a youngish widower with a relative, Mrs Frith, a rather formidable elderly lady, as his housekeeper. There was a good-natured middle-aged Matron, always known as the Duck, and lots of domestic staff.

Jacob's great interest was his scheme of splitting up the boys into Leagues, each with a Captain and Vice-Captain. This was linked to a system of Plus and Minus or League points which covered every aspect of school life. A boy gained Plus points for good work in class, alertness to others' needs, politeness and good performance in all sports and games, etc, etc. Minus points were for lateness, untidy habits or dress, dirty ears or fingernails, rowdy behaviour and noise, and much more.

All this was balanced up weekly and put on a large display board and the group total declared.

In support of the points system Jacob had a sheet of table manners printed and given to all. This also served as copy for writing lines, if this was incurred as a punishment.

He much disliked untidy bootlaces, and introduced a method of lacing our boots with a single lace, the end being tucked into the boot.

Standing with hands in pockets was also taboo, as was sucking fingers or pencils, etc. Bad offenders were given a baby's dummy to be hung around the neck for the rest of the day.

Jacob was a user of shorthand. Books or papers handed out were often marked with a very small shorthand of the boy's name. If found lying around, it would be returned along with a number of minus points.

Tennis: Jacob was a very keen tennis player, and we used to watch

14

him from the classroom windows playing with his friends on his tennis courts – the present lawn behind the main block. In his usual methodical way he was also seen digging out weeds from the court early each morning. He also practised service strokes into the back nets.

Swimming: Jacob took us over to the School Swimming baths weekly and usually went himself into the water. At the deep end there was a high diving board (This was taken down for safety reasons in the '60s). He would challenge a boy, even a non-swimmer, to go up and jump in while he was swimming around to fish him out. If you did this jump, you got sixpence and a lot of plus points for your first jump.

Gym: We went once a week to the School Gym and did all the usual things on the bars, horse and rope climbing, etc. Jacob encouraged boxing, and to start off the small boys the School Gym Sergeant used to squat down to the little boy's level and let him have a few punches at the man's head! Again plus points for anything done in the Gym.

Press-Ups: On getting up in the morning the boys had to do six press-ups on the dormitory floor, supervised by the League Captain. As a dayboy I did this at home.

Names: Christian names were never used by anyone, only surnames but with nicknames in addition. One's friends were Smith minor or Tubby Jones or just plain Robinson. The Headmaster both of Felsted and at the Prep was always 'The Old Man'.

'Going Up': At about 12 or 13 Jacob would get a boy to his study – all surrounded with his Rugger photos and Caps – and have a talk about matters of sex, etc, both moral and physical. After prayer one was asked to join in a Bond of Purity and given a promise card to keep pure in both body and mind, which one was asked to sign with him and keep for the future. This was known as 'Going Up' among the boys.

Felsted Words – used in Prep and Big School

Dips – electric lights, coming from use of dipped wax candles.

Dips out – bedtime.

Duck – Matron. San Duck – Infirmary nurse

Fug up – wrap up in cold weather.

Fug pipes – radiators, usually long hot water pipes.

Bogs, shants – W C Shanty, an old Essex word for shed or outdoor loo.

Hots – pennies or other coins. Hot in the pocket and soon spent. Please can you lend me a hot?

In 1910 the lease of the Junior House property expired, and the school was bought from the Millers for £4,450. 'The school has purchased during the year the Junior House, which was built by Mr Miller, its first Housemaster. . . . The Junior House has been so prosperous during the last three years under Mr Jacob that it seemed wise to seize the opportunity of making it School property.' Felstedian November 1910.

Jacob's wife had died not long after his appointment. They had no children. Shortly after the outbreak of war, in the Christmas holidays of 1914/15 he married Mrs Frith, who had been acting as his housekeeper. 'On December 18th we had our break-up supper. The occasion was important owing to the approaching marriage of Mr Jacob and Mrs Frith. . . . At the close of the feast two presentations were made – one by Dixon and Hopkins on behalf of the Old Preptonians in the School and the other by Rippon on behalf of the House.' J H Report, Felstedian February 1914. Mrs Frith was comfortably off and spent much of her wealth on furnishing the 'Private' side of the Prep.

At the school, until the beginning of 1917, the 'Great War' had effected few changes, although there was the steady flow of reports of casualties. The May 1917 Felstedian reported 'Sports prizes are made of paper not silver; there is a scarcity of younger masters and older boys (at eighteen one feels quite ancient); but otherwise everything has been much the same. But this term everything is different. To begin with our food is rationed out to us; we do not eat in the old, careless way; eating is now reduced to a science of calories, of pounds and of ounces. Secondly, work on the land in term time is in full swing, and the purpose for which we are primarily sent here has for the moment taken second place. Even the boys of the Junior House went pea-picking and dock-pulling, and potatoes were grown in the League gardens instead of flowers and strawberries.' And 'the War has made fewer changes in the personnel and routine of the Junior House than it has elsewhere. Its chief result is that nearly all the members are trying hard to decide whether they ought to eventually adorn the Army, the Navy or the Royal Flying Corps.'

Much of the material for life at the Prep. in the later years of Jacob's reign has been drawn from the recollections of H.E. Walker who was there from 1924 to 1928. He assesses Jacob's character in these words.

'Jock', as he was known to the boys, or 'Jakie', as he was known to some of the village folk, was certainly a formidable character....
He was stern, inflexible and totally honest. He was also humourless,

16

devoid of human warmth and, in many ways, an ass. On the credit side, the boys were reliable, responsible and well behaved, and there was hardly ever any bullying.

As a teacher he was quite exceptionally bad. Jock took French and nothing else for Divisions IV to I inclusive (I was the top Division). French preparation never varied from the day I arrived in Division IV to the day I left in Division I. We had to learn the parts of one verb for each prep, starting with 'avoir' and 'etre', then doing the four regular conjugations, followed by the same set of irregular verbs up to the end of term. The next morning the verb had to be written out in a standard manner – everything was standardised. Every lesson was organised in the same way. The front bench was turned back, so that eight boys sat on it, while the rest stood up, making a sort of oval with Jacob at his desk at one end. Each boy had to perform. If he made a mistake, he had to go down a place. Sometimes Jock threw out an unexpected question, and if the boy didn't answer it correctly, it would be passed on to the next boy, and so on, until some bright lad got the right answer. It was a bit like a Christmas party game, but without the fun. . . . There was never any study of French grammar, nor any French conversation, nor any translation from English into French.

Much of the teaching of non-academic subjects was also mechanical and repetitious. For instance, Carpentry, which took up one hour every week as long as a boy was at the Prep. Each term he had to make five standard joints which never varied, irrespective of which Division he was in. Mr. Wood, the school Carpenter, awarded marks for these joints, but they were credited not to the boy but to his League, as carpentry was one of the League competitions. Not surprisingly, the boys became bored and lost interest in what could have been an enjoyable part of their practical education. However, if a boy had completed his joints well before the end of term, Mr Wood would help him to construct something worthwhile such as a box – using the joints.

'Gym' was also subject to the same repetition during the Monday and Friday afternoon visits there. There were three activities and three groups of about fifteen boys in each, based on ability. One group used the vaulting horse, another group the horizontal bar and the third group did boxing under Sergeant Ebert. Jacob and either Tomlinson or Davies took the two gymnastics groups. Each period there were two kinds of activity on a rota system, horse-and-bar, bar-and-boxing or boxing-and-horse. On the horse and bar the exercises never varied from year to year or from

17

group to group, whatever their ability, and the same inflexible routine tended to become very tedious.

THE LEAGUE POINTS SYSTEM

Plus-points were awarded for a number of activities, and there was a two page notice giving details of what they were. One sheet consisted solely of gymnastic exercises so that a good gymnast was at an immediate advantage. These points could only be claimed if judged and passed by a League Captain. Other plus points were given so:

> Daily exercises in the dormitory night and morning (6 leg-ups, 6 press-ups) – 10 points.
> Compulsory cold shower every morning – 5 points in the Summer and 10 points in the Christmas and Easter terms.
> Swimming: four lengths of the baths, compulsory for all swimmers – 15 points, diving off the 6 foot board, complusory for all divers – 5 points. These to be done every day. In addition, 20 lengths of the baths could be done once a term for 100 points.
> Winning a League match – 30 points for the winning side.
> Coming top of the class (weekly) – 30 points.
> Killing a queen wasp or mouse – 5 points.
> Points were also awarded for winning a bout in the inter-League boxing or wrestling competition or a heat in the swimming competition.
> Coming top of an activity on the Challenge Board at a certain date at the end of term.

Minus points were deducted for various misdemeanours but, unlike plus points, there were no rules nor any notices on the board. One had to learn by trial and error. Each new boy had an older one to look after him for the first week. He was meant to explain the do's and don'ts. The scale of minus points was never disclosed, but most crimes merited -40, except for 'leaving anything about' which cost -5. Every night Jacob wandered around the house after the boys were in bed collecting anything which had not been put away. These objects had to be claimed by lunch time on pocket money day. If any item was left unclaimed, then nobody got any pocket money that week. Jacob kept a termly record of 'things left about'. Twenty items was the limit without incurring extra punishment, and the annual report to parents included an item – 'things left about'.

Every Sunday morning the Headmaster came over to read out the points. If a boy got 100 minus points or less, there was no further punishment. Minus 105-300 meant losing Wednesday's half holiday. Over 300 put the boy on the 'blacklist' which entailed additional punishment, such as not being allowed to eat any tuck (including jam for breakfast and supper) throughout the following week. Jacob always carried with him a little plastic aide-memoire in which he kept jotting down minus points. A boy could go through the term virtually unpunished, but Jacob's constant vigilance for minor offences could be decidedly irksome.

Apart from losing points there were additional punishments which included:

> Copybook – each boy had a copybook to improve his writing, but it was used only as a punishment.
> Pumping – in Jacob's garden there was a well with a pump which could be used to augment the water supply.
> Stones – there were League gardens just inside the main gate. A boy could spend 15 minutes collecting stones, the size of a walnut or bigger, and putting them on a permanent heap near the gate.
> Stumping – for slovenly posture. A cricket stump was placed for twenty minutes across a boy's back with arms hooked over so as to draw the shoulders back.
> Whacking-off – instead of carrying out these various tasks a boy could opt for two strokes of the cane. Proper beatings were given for crimes which Jacob considered serious. One didn't yell; this was expected of a brave young knight. Four of Jacob's best was decidedly painful.

> 'The Challenge Board' was a large board bearing about ten columns, each concerning some form of activity. Each column consisted of small cards inscribed with the boys' names in their League colours. There were columns for 'efficiency', work, chess, draughts, high and long jump, running, swimming and throwing the cricket ball. The three major games and boxing and wrestling were not included. In theory the idea of the challenge was that any boy could challenge any other boy above him on the ladder. In practice, there was very little challenging because, in many cases, it was not possible.

'Efficiency' referred to individual League order, work to class order, both at the end of the previous term, so that in effect there could be no challenge during the term. High and long jump and the cricket ball depended on annual events, each held on a full afternoon in the Summer term. Running depended on the annual steeplechase and had nothing to do with sprinting, relay races or the 'mile', run every year at the start of the Summer term.

Virtually the only acitivities for which a challenge was possible were chess, draughts or swimming, for which there were League competitions, but 'A' could only challenge 'B' once a term.

The earlier reference to 'Going Up' needs further explanation. There was a 'League of Manlinesss' which every boy was supposed to join soon after his 12th birthday. After an interview with Jacob in his study, he signed a book with red covers, which still exists in the School archives, and from them on he was vowed to 'personal purity'. H E Walker describes the occasion as it happened for him.

> When I entered the Prep. after three years at St. Aubyn's my little head was stuffed fairly well with Latin, French and Maths, but I was terribly ignorant about life in general, completely un-streetwise and totally ignorant of all matters sexual, in spite of being moderately interest in Natural History. . . . I never heard any mention of the League of Manliness until it was my turn to be roped into it.
>
> One Sunday, several months after my twelfth birthday, Jacob came up to me after Chapel and asked to see me in his study. I duly reported, and was led into his house where he deposited me at one side of his dining room table. He then gave me a pamphlet to read, while he sat opposite and glowered from the other side of the table. I read through a tract of gobbledegook all about purity of mind, body and spirit. I well remember a quotation from Sir Galahad, 'my strength is as the strength of ten, because my heart is pure'. . . . I felt sure that Jock was getting at me for something horrible that I had done, and I was on the verge of tears. Towards the end of the homily on purity there was a brief reference to bird life and a mention of how, in the mating season, birds' eggs were made fertile. This I thought was an interesting bit of Natural History, but by that time I was feeling somewhat bemused and benumbed.
>
> When I had finished reading the pamphlet Jock boomed at me, 'Do you understand it?' (He never spoke, he always boomed). I at once replied, 'No', whereupon he gave me a resumé of what I had already read on the subject of purity. As I was none the wiser, I decided it was best just to shut up. He handed me his card which contained the rules and aims of the League of Manliness, and handed me a book which he asked me to sign. Until that moment I had not only never heard of the League, but

I therefore promise that I will refrain, with God's help, from all impurity or indecency in my talk and in my actions, and that I will endeavour bravely and tactfully to prevent it in others.

Name_____

Date_____

———

Prayer to be used daily.

ALMIGHTY God, who hatest all impurity, and has taught us that only the pure in heart can see Thee, look down upon my weakness; make me a clean heart and a right spirit within me; help me this day to drive out every evil thought, to conquer every evil desire. Lead us not into temptation, but deliver us from evil, for Christ's sake. Amen.

FELSTED SCHOOL.

The League of Manliness.

✿

WEAKNESS is wretchedness! To be strong
Is to be happy!
The Golden Legend—Longfellow.

———

QUIT you like men and fight.
I. Sam., iv., 9.

———

AND doubly cursed my failing brand!
A sinful heart makes feeble hand.
Marmion—Sir Walter Scott.

———

MY good blade carves the casques of men,
My tough lance thrustest sure,
My strength is as the strength of ten
Because my heart is pure.
Sir Galahad—Lord Tennyson.

Q. Why should I keep myself pure in mind and body?

A. 1. Because impure thoughts lead to impure actions.—*James i., 15.*

2. Because impurity of body destroys my will and power to do what is right.
Judges xvi., 20.

3. Because it undermines my health, ruins my moral nature, and soon becomes a habit which I cannot break off.
Rev. xxii., 11.

4. Because my body is the temple of God.
I. Cor. iii., 16, 17; vi., 19.

5. Because if I am impure I set an example which will be followed by others.
vid. St. Luke xvii., 2 (R.V.)

6. Because if I yield to impurity, I am a traitor to my house, my school, and my country.

Figure 2: Booklet given to those who joined the League of Manliness. Top: front and back covers. Below: centre pages.

he had never even mentioned it to me by name. Anyway, I signed the book and noticed that some other contemporaries of mine had also signed it before me, so I derived some comfort from knowing that, whatever foul deed I had committed, had also been committed by them.

I presume that it was partly Jacob's idea of giving his charges some idea of the facts of life. As far as I was concerned, his attempt was so oblique that it was a complete failure.

Jacob's moralising was remarkably effective, and the boys were, on the whole, truthful, honest and responsible. Every now and then there would be a 'raid' which usually took place at lunchtime when the boys were all gathered together in the dining hall. Before Grace he would ask, 'What boys have been doing…?' or 'Who was responsible for…?' It very seldom occurred that a boy failed to own up, whether he was alone or a member of a group.

Jacob was also very keen on constantly inspecting things. On Sundays it was four cards, 'A guide to Happiness' which contained some admirable but somewhat idealistic rules of behaviour, 'Hints on Table Manners', and in the two Winter terms, 'Practice Games' and 'Tackling' which consisted of rules, hints and advice for Rugger. This was at breakfast; at lunchtime it was always the boys' teeth, fingernails and boot or shoe laces. Every weekday caps were inspected at lunchtime to check that each boy had his own. There were other regular inspections for other pieces of clothing.

There was also the 'all correct' routine. There were various details imposed on one's dress, such as the tiepin and the tie clip which also had to be in place. Every French lesson taken by Jacob commenced with the question, 'Anybody not all correct?' This covered the dress requirements and various other duties such as daily exercises and showers.

In 1924 Jacob married for the third time, Mrs Cecil, who brought her two daughters and a son, Robin, who was a pupil at the Prep. 'We welcome to Felsted Mrs Jacob and Mrs (Elsie) Thorne and also the two masters who join the staff this term, Mr Lockwood and Mr Day.' Felstedian November 1924. It later became understood that the three figures in the stained glass window in Chapel referred to the three wives of Jacob. This window was removed when the Chapel was enlarged. The stained glass was not kept.

1 The football team of 1900.

2 From a prospectus of between 1900 and 1903. The tennis court is now the 'quad' or car park.

3 The 'Tin-Gym'.

4 Dr Frith in 1906, his last complete year as head of the Junior House. The boys' suits show a great variety of styles – no uniform here yet.

5 Jacob with the League Captains. Undated, but probably within five years of his appointment in 1907.

6 July 1912. Next to Jacob is Mrs Frith. On his left is W A Tomlinson, on her right is T Cooper. K Turner, whose recollections are included in the section on Jacob, stands 4th row from the top, 2nd from left.

7 Gaselee League. First winners of the
St George and Dragon Efficiency
Trophy, December 1907. General Sir
Alfred Gaselee's photograph is
displayed below the trophy.

8 W A Tomlinson – "Tommy".

9 The New Wing of 1934.

10 General view of the Junior School with the new wing shortly after completion in September 1934.

11 Canon ffrome Court, home to
the Junior House from June
1940 to July 1945.

12 O I Simpson.

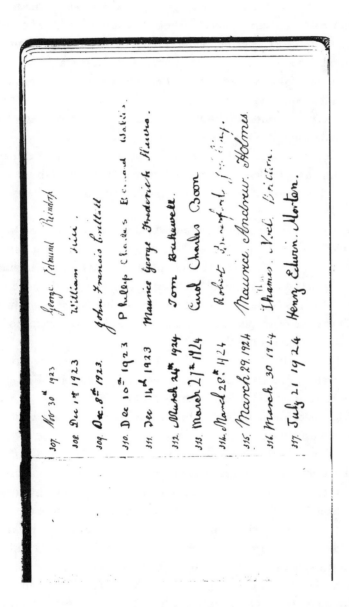

Figure 3: A specimen page from the book of the League of Manliness. Signatures include those of the future Bishop Reindorp, J F Crittall, who was to be Chairman of the Governors of Felsted School and Sir Maurice Holmes, Governor.

H E Walker recalls the third Mrs Jacob as being, 'one of the nicest, finest and most charming persons whom I have ever met'. She had a tremendous influence over life at the Prep., although largely from the background. One of her ideas was to introduce League teas. The Jacobs invited one boy from each of the five Leagues to tea in their house on Tuesday afternoons, in League order, until all the boys had been invited. After tea there was a putting competition on the drawing room carpet, the prize for the winner being sixpence.

Robin Cecil was Captain of Cricket at the Prep., went on to Wellington College and Caius College, Cambridge – with scholarships at both – and enjoyed a distinguished career as a diplomat and historian. He died in 1994.

In 1923 the land now known as Follyfield was bought for the Junior House with the possibility of a new Senior School House being built on the site. Indeed Follyfield House was opened in 1929. 'The remainder of the Folly Field has been put down to grass, and owing to the assiduous labours of Mr Jacob the impossible has been achieved, and the Junior House boys are already playing on what will henceforth be their football grounds.' Felstedian November 1928.

Over the road 1930 was marked by the destruction of the original Grignon Hall by fire, and also by the death of Col Philpott OF who left the Bury House and its gardens to the School in his will.

In 1932 there died, tragically before his time, a master who had spanned almost the same length of time at the Junior House as Jacob himself. He was W A Tomlinson, who arrived in 1910, and came to be Jacob's right hand man. He died in February of that year after two operations for appendicitis. A good disciplinarian and very conscientious schoolmaster, he had a number of hobbies which he shared with the boys, one of which was story collecting and telling, a source of great joy to his friends. He was a quiet and unassuming man, popular not only with the boys and with his colleagues, but also with the non-academic employees of the school and with the people of the village. He is the 'Tommy' of Peter Church's account in Appendix 2. H E Walker remembers him,

> He was a Classics man who also knew Spanish and Arabic. He taught us Divinity and took the lower Divisions for Maths. He was one of the most ascetic men I ever knew. So much so that he carried

on a mild but continuous propaganda campaign against over-eating, which made us ashamed of having 'a jolly good gut'. Even so, as master in charge of Hockey at the Prep., he always stood the XI a substantial tea in the village tearoom at the end of the Easter term. . . . During World War I he joined the Army and remained a Private until the Armistice, although I am sure that he could have obtained a commission. . . . His experience of the food dished out to the men in the trenches probably accounts for the fact that he could always eat whatever was put in front of him in the Prep. dining room.

The other member of staff, whose time at the Prep. (1916-32) covered most of the Jacob years was H R St A Davies, known to the boys as 'Dove'. He was in charge of Cricket and Rugger and taught History, Geography and Divinity. Like 'Tommy' he was a kindly man and was well liked by the boys. He used to invite boys, two at a time, to breakfast at his home opposite the station on Sundays. 'I remember being invited on a bitterly cold day one winter. The breakfast was most enjoyable, but it meant a long walk there and back, arriving just in time for Chapel.'

Some masters from the Senior School taught at the Prep. They included J R E Howard, one lesson of Botany per week. This was much enjoyed, but not included in the end-of-term exams. T Cooper, housemaster of Stocks', took the two top Divisions for all Maths and Divisions III and IV for Geometry. 'He was a martinet with a temper, and we were all scared of him. His teaching was rigorous and he certainly got results.' D H Morgan, nicknamed 'Daddy Morgan' by the Prep. boys, was in charge of Engineering at the Senior School and took the whole Prep. for one hour per week in freehand drawing. This was used as a basis of one of the many League competitions, and marks were handed in at the end of the term. George Thorne was the music master. There was one hour each week of community singing for the whole Prep. together, and he also taught piano to the few boys who took it as an extra. The Prep. had one hour a week with Mr. Wood, the School carpenter. It also formed the basis of a League competition each term. Finally there was Sergeant Ebert who took the Prep. for one hour's P T every Tuesday, for boxing in the gym on Mondays and Fridays and for swimming lessons for the non-swimmers. Very little was taught rigorously, apart from Cooper's Maths and Tomlinson's Latin.

When he retired in 1933, Jacob went off the Srinagar in Kashmir to start a new career in Tyndale Biscoe's school, devoting himself to the education of Indian children. Biscoe shared Jacob's views on manliness and he was enthusiastically welcomed.

It is interesting to note that as far back as June 1910 a lecture was given by Rev Tyndale Biscoe in the Laboratory of Felsted School entitled 'Character Building in Kashmir'. After speaking of the superstitions of the Kashmiris and their subservience to the fakirs and to their cowardice after centuries of cruelty at the hands of tyrants, he showed slides illustrating the change he had made during 19 years work at his school. 'His object was not so much to convert the boys as to instil some feelings of common decency and cleanliness into them and to teach them to show respect to women, who were very badly treated in Kashmir.' He wrote a book entitled 'Character-building in Kashmir', showing how much his ideas were similar to those of Jacob, but Jacob did not meet him until they met at Felsted in 1919.

In another lecture at Felsted just after the War Biscoe spoke of how he, a Cambridge Blue, had introduced swimming and rowing to his boys and how a number of them could swim across a great lake five miles wide. Was this the same lake of the same width across which Jacob swam, at the age of 78, shortly before his death in 1945?

The appreciation of Jacob's work written in the Felstedian on his retirement from the Junior House is given in Appendix 1. A further account of the School under Jacob also appears as an Appendix. It was written by P.J.B. Church and appeared in the Autumn 1954 Young Felstedian.

3

Andrew C Telfer
1933 – 1946

The last appointment which Frank Stephenson made as Headmaster was to bring back Andrew Telfer from Ludlow to succeed Jacob at the Junior House. Telfer had originally joined the Staff at Felsted in 1920. At Cambridge before the war he had been a Cross Country Blue and was first President of the Cambridge University Athletics Club after the war. At Felsted he was in charge of Rugger and Running. In 1927 he had left to become Headmaster of Ludlow Grammar School.

After 26 years at the Junior House Jacob may have felt some reluctance to leave, for when the Telfers arrived to take over, they found that the only possessions to have found their way into the packing cases was a set of golf clubs. Mrs Telfer recalls that, when they eventually moved in, the non-teaching staff included the Matron, a lady cook called Miss Wakeham, a Nanny for their daughter Mary and 10 resident maids.

The new Headmaster of Felsted was the Rev Julian Bickersteth MC, who had been Headmaster of St Peter's College, Adelaide, Australia since 1919. At his first Speech Day he was able to announce a major expansion of the Junior House. Jacob had left it full with 50 boys, but space was cramped. In the J H Magazine of Easter 1934 Telfer wrote:

> The school has been divided into four forms, instead of the old three, and forms have been redivided for Latin, French and Mathematics. A boy need not be kept back in other subjects

now because of weakness in one. As we have only three classrooms on the premises, we are using what was the Museum in the Old School House. This has relieved pressure a bit; but the classroom accommodation is still inadequate. We are very glad, therefore, to be able to announce that the building of the new wing will start this holiday.

The block has been designed by two OFs, Messrs Chetwood and Grant, and the contractors also know the school, as they built the new Grignon Hall.

The main features of the additions – a full south aspect for the classrooms, cross ventilation, lavatories with hot and cold water for each dormitory and a dignified Dining Hall to seat 80 persons. It will be possible to open the whole south side of the classrooms so that they become practically open air rooms, looking out on to the turf. [The cloister arches, through which one could walk out on to 'Cloisterfield', were bricked to waist height and glazed in 1982.] The Dining Hall will have a dais, and opening from it will be a room which can be used as a green-room when plays are performed in the Hall. There will be a real School Door [now the Red Doors] with an entrance hall inside where we can meet our people, instead of having to meet them among the dustbins as at present. There will be another set of Master's rooms and a Common Room right in the middle of things, and three dormitories over the classrooms. We are doubling accommodation and so shall be able to increase our numbers by about fifty per cent. [The – very small – Common Room was gathered into the entrance lobby in 1983.] The new block will be ready by September, and high speed building will be going on all next term. Entry to the playing fields and to the 'Private Side' will be by a new drive alongside the League Tennis Courts.

A hockey quadrangle (which also served as a roller skating rink) was made in front of the main building. It was in use for 'Quad Hockey' until the 1980s when the deterioration of the surface and the increasing use of the space as a car park made it impracticable.

The Junior House could now take 80 boys, divided into six forms, and by September 1936 there were five graduate assistant masters. That year the fees were rationalised in both the Senior and Junior parts of the school. The cost per annum of keeping a boy at the Junior House was £140, the same as at School House. Fees at Elwyn's and Follyfield, the two Out Houses, were higher at £150. In spite of the slump of the 1930s numbers kept up.

Jacob's system of plus and minus points was retained on a more restricted basis, and academic work which had taken second place to character building previously, began to improve. In his Speech of 1939 Headmaster Bickersteth said that,

> . . . he was glad to report a steady improvement in the standard of work at the Junior House. For the first time for a good many years two boys, J H F Malleson and J R Neal, obtained places on the short list in the Open Scholarship Entrance Examination.

What was life like at the Junior House in the five or six years before war broke out again? The following account was written in 1970 by some of the older boys as a result of interviewing Telfer.

THE JUNIOR SCHOOL UNDER THE REVD A C TELFER
1933 – 46

When Mr. Telfer took over in 1933, the Junior House consisted of what are now the old gym – the green painted, corrugated iron structure which was put up in 1909 and replaced by the Ross Hall in 1970, the lavatories, the passage with ablutions – which comprised 8 iron wash basins jutting out in a Penthouse from the passage – the changing rooms and the new common room. The only dormitories were Cromwell passage, Smythies, Gaselee and X dormitory. Where Wilson (built in 1947, demolished in 1993 to make way for a two storey classroom extension to the Telfer wing) now stands, there was a Gardening Patch for boys who wished to garden. Where the quad now is, there were some grass Tennis Courts.

The boys, of whom a great majority were boarders, had a tough life, except for the League Captains who had far more authority than they have today. In fact the League Captains practically kept the house in running order, for often there was no master in the House. In the morning an ordinary boy had to do certain duties. When the bell rang, he had to jump out of bed, say his prayers, have a cold bath, then go to the window and take 10 deep breaths! When you were dressing you had to remember what day it was so that you could put the right tie on, because two days of the week you had to wear a blue one, another two days you had to put on a League tie and on the remaining two days you had to wear the School tie. On Sundays the black Sunday tie was worn. Further, your shoe laces had to be tied up in the special Jacob knot!

As far as the rest of the day was concerned, there was Prep for the whole School before going to Chapel. Then for the periods up to lunch, it was all the same as it is now. Lunch was held in the present Common Room, so you can imagine the squash making 60-80 boys eat in that room. Each League had its own table and the Leagues moved round each week. In the afternoon they always changed to get some exercise. The usual games were played, the most popular being Rugby. Hockey was also popular amongst the boys and the great attraction of the Hockey season was the game against the 'Chelmsford Ladies' which was held annually. The boys were always anxious to win this match and it was a great achievement if they did. If it was too wet to play games, boys were sent on runs, more often than not round the' three', Mr. Telfer pacing them on his bicycle. If you were physically unable to play games, you were not known as 'OFF EX' as you are today but as 'AEGER' from the Latin and if you were ill enough to go to the Sanatorium, you were looked after by the 'INVADUCK', as the Matron was then called. In the evening the 'Upper School' had a second prep, and League Duties were inspected by the League Captains who made sure that they were done efficiently. If some labour was not to their satisfaction, a League Captain would punish the miscreant. A favourite torture was to make a boy jump up onto the gym door whereupon the door was slammed – causing considerable discomfort.

When Mr Jacob left off as Headmaster, Mr. Telfer was asked whether he would carry on the points system, which he duly did ... for a short time! You were given minus points for the following:
-40 for 'Being late' or 'Anything Mangy'
-30 for 'Losing anything', 'Hands in side pockets' or 'Not doing your League Duty'
-20 for 'Forgetting', 'A mistake in correcting' or 'Giving up the wrong marks in form'
-10 was the reward for 'Clumsiness', 'Nail biting', 'Pen sucking' or 'Bad manners'. Whereas 'Untidy laces', 'Carelessness' or 'Dropping anything' – less serious offences – received a meagre -5.

This was the debit side of things. The way to obtain points was to perform a sensible task, a description of which you wrote down on paper and placed in the 'claims box'. If you did an exceptionally useful task and thought it was worth +80, your paper was taken to the Headmaster who inspected it to see if it was in fact worth +80. There was one boy who, when Cloisterfield had to have stones removed from it for grass sowing, picked up twenty stones, for which he received +5. The stones he placed in a tin. The next day he carefully poured the same stones out and picked them up again claiming a further five points. Eventually this fiendish plan was discovered by the regularity of the boy claiming +5, and he was stopped.

If by saintliness or cunning you did not receive -100 in any one week, you would go to the Headmaster and be presented with 6d; but if you had more you were taken up to the highest room in the

house and there beaten. It was very rare a boy ever had under
-100. This points system was eventually stopped by Mr Waters,
who found it far too troublesome to write out hundreds of noughts
each week when going through the League Points.

In 1933 when Mr. Telfer became Headmaster, the standard of
work was appalling. There were three masters, Mr. Telfer, Mr
Andrew (who spent 2 years at the J H, 8 years at the Senior School,
was recalled from war service to become Headmaster in 1943, and
died tragically in 1947) and Mr Payne, and consequently three
forms. Very few boys indeed ever passed the Common Entrance
Examination. The whole school used one large timetable, instead
of using a timetable for each form. In 1933 Mr. Telfer experimented
by bringing an extra subject, Science, to the boys' attention. The
drawback to this was that the equipment had to be brought over
from the Senior School at the beginning of the period and taken
back at the end. So Science was eventually stopped. However, in
1939, the standard had risen and the House was able to put forward
its first candidates for the Scholarship Examination.

War broke out on September 3rd 1939, and Telfer wrote in the
Christmas issue of the magazine about how it had changed life at the
Junior House.

This has been a curious time but definitely a happy one in spite
of the abnormal times. On the outbreak of war all staff returned,
and the school was opened to receive boys living in supposedly
dangerous areas. Until they returned Smythies dormitory housed
two evacuee families until billets could be found for them. The
Masters set to work to 'black out' our 179 windows, and the result
of their labours has proved very satisfactory. Ten days before term
officially began we opened up Smythies again for Captain Ames and
his temporary league of refugees. It was lovely weather and 'a good
time was had by all'.

The war seems to us very remote, and we have had no air
raid warnings. We have concrete shelters to which we may go if
incendiary bombs are used. It is difficult to get transport for 'away'
matches, visitors are much fewer and we have started a modified
system of rationing as part of an anti-waste campaign. Otherwise the
life of the school goes on as usual. The introduction of the rationing
raised a grumble by the more voracious, and a notice in a hand we
recognised, proclaimed, 'We want more of everything'.

On further investigation it was discovered that 'everything' was
not intended to include work.

The national rationing scheme which will be in force next term will entail a lot of extra work but, as we are registered as a 'catering establishment', we are not expecting to pull belts in yet.

One interesting phenomenon of the term has been the noticeably smaller number of coughs and colds. Can it be that fresh air fiends are wrong after all and the stuffiness of the 'black-out' nights is like Guinness?

Fortunately we ordered our timber for the Hobby House last term and got it just before the supply was restricted. The frame, roof and windows are now done and we should be able to use the House next term.

The Hobby House was the result of gifts of money and materials from a number of parents. It still stands as the shingle-roofed, wooden building adjacent to the old coach house and facing onto Cloisterfield. After an undignified period as the boys' bootroom and storeroom, it was re-roofed and re-equipped for a use closer to its original function. It is now the CDT room.

Five months after the extract above was written, just after Sports Day in May 1940, the Telfers were given 10 days notice to quit the Junior House premises to make room for the Army and to find other accommodation for the school. The Senior School went to Hill Court, to the larger Goodrich Court and to Pencraig Court, all within two or three miles of one another and all owned by Mrs Trafford, a good friend of Headmaster Bickersteth. Telfer set off for the West Country with Olaf Simpson, and after much driving around they came to Canon ffrome Court which was near Ledbury and about 20 miles from Ross-on-Wye, the town near which were situated the houses occupied by the Senior School. This geographical separation from the main school was to have a profound effect on the way the Junior House managed its affairs and developed a feeling of independence and self-sufficiency. Indeed, this isolation was to lead to the Junior House becoming the Junior School with a Headmaster instead of a Housemaster, with membership of the IAPS. These words written in the Junior House notes for the Felstedian have a prophetic ring about them:

...But, if there is one thing that stands out after a year and a half at Canon ffrome, it is that there is among us a growing feeling of independence and self-assertion; I mean we are all thrown on our own resources so much more, and have so much more free time in which to amuse ourselves; and there seems something in Herefordshire that was wanting in Essex, an air of spaciousness and expanse which the Junior House proper lacked. . . . So we proceed on our way, still an integral part of Felsted, somewhat more independent than we used to be, necessarily, but still the Junior House, and, who knows, we may sow seeds in the West which will bear much fruit in the future.

Canon ffrome Court was owned by Mrs Hopton and was already under threat of requisition for evacuees from Birmingham. In 1786 a Richard Hopton pulled down the house which an ancestor built when the 'Strong House' with its moat was destroyed in the Civil War. The new house was completed in 1789, and it had been recently modernised before the Junior House moved in. It was probably the most suitable of all the houses for use as a school. A large Music Room was used for assemblies and concerts. There was a lake in front of the house and a 1,500 yard rifle range built by Colonel Hopton, a fanatical shot, who was buried by the firing point. Twenty yards away was the parish church of Canon ffrome, although there was no longer a village, enclosures having forced it outside the park. The church, by the kindness of the Vicar, was used as the School Chapel both for Sunday services and daily prayer. The Junior House had found a home from home:

> In a surprisingly short time things were working smoothly and well; bathe (in the lake) before breakfast for showers, cricket on the village ground (two and a half miles away) and such changes were quickly accepted; even the Tuck Shop started to function. Bicycles are a great blessing and those who have a licence, i.e. who have passed an easy test, go for many excursions. The cricketers are torn between their own game and the unaccustomed freedom a bicycle bestows; but they have concentrated enough on the former to win two matches – so far!
>
> In front of the house we do archery, near the lake, which is never more than four feet deep except where there was once a monks' fish pond; and on the island there are many wild ducks and geese. The estate carpenter teaches carpentry; we have plenty of fun and exercise; in fact, the only drawback to Canon ffrome is the war – yet this was the cause of our coming here, and, for that, we are very grateful.

Anne Telfer went into the 1st Form, and her sister Mary started her schooling with the local doctor. They were the first girl pupils at the Prep. until 1992. Until the Spring of 1943 when he resigned, the Headmaster, Julian Bickersteth, came over every Wednesday from Ross-on-Wye to visit the Junior House. With him came George Thorne and Miss Joan Nield to teach Music and 'Arge' Ebert to give instruction in Boxing and P.T. Telfer's staff included Maj. C P Sparrow, M C G Hooton and O I Simpson. Hooton, who had joined Telfer in 1936, brought the boys up to a high standard in competitive archery at Canon ffrome. He moved to the Senior School after the return to Felsted. Mrs Telfer recalls the time when he mounted guard with the Home Guard at Col. Hopton's monument on the occasion of a 'scare'.

Olaf Simpson joined the Junior House staff at the same time as Hooton, and like him went to teach at the Senior School. After his retirement he returned occasionally to the Prep to help out with Classics teaching, bringing with him his King Charles spaniel 'Rowley'.

On the domestic side were Miss Wakeham, the cook, the Matron, and four maids from Felsted whose wages were £52 per annum. Mrs Telfer remembers how difficult the catering was to start with, until the school was changed from being a 'catering establishment' to an 'institution'. Jams and sugar were placed in individually named pots around the League tables, but this did not stop one member of staff helping himself to the boys' jam rations! It was especially difficult to provide 'spreads' for the morning and afternoon breaks.

In 1943 Telfer was ordained, following in the footsteps of his father who was also a clergyman. As Mrs Telfer remarked, it did make it easier to run the spiritual side of the school, especially the organisation of services.

Two final extracts from the J H Notes written by Olaf Simpson will round off this account of life in Herefordshire during the war.

> Our vast Music Room has been in use as a theatre, where on Saturdays the Leagues have been amusing us in turn.
>
> We heard a siren one night, but it was from Malvern, and we only heard it because the wind was coming that way. We have stirrup pumps and sand on two roofs and fire squads who have been through their duties. It is fun to play with water legally! And the other Sunday the Ashperton AFS came out to test their hoses and our water supply, with very satisfactory results ....

We appreciate the peace and quiet of this place enormously and are well established now, and we think, not unpopular in the neighbourhood. In many ways we shall be sorry to leave when the time comes.

It is curious that the possibilities of organised games are much rarer than at home, but we seem quite able to do things without creating damage either to ourselves or to local property. At Felsted the bounds, though invisible, were very definite; whereas here there are no places to put permanently out of bounds. Consequently we are freer, in one sense, to go abroad.

Perhaps the most appreciated part of the estate is the lake. We have built a diving board over the very deep part, and that gives us an excuse to go on to the island; and it is a grand place for sailing yachts. Moreover, more people are learning to swim and dive than ever did at Felsted.

Generally we may be described as being in a happy place, and though it may sound the wrong word to use (but I don't think it is) we are, really, enjoying it.

As the years went by the Junior House established a strong local connection; it was always full and boys from Essex mingled with those from the West of England. The local inhabitants, from the Station Master to the Estate workmen were very friendly and kind; the farmers, particularly those whose hops and potatoes the Junior House helped to gather, were not too grumbly.
From: 'Felsted in Herefordshire'

This rural idyll could not last forever. In May 1945 the Senior School reopened back in Felsted, but the Junior House stayed on one more term in Herefordshire, moving back in August and bidding farewell 'to the Court, to all our friends, and to Mrs Hopton especially, with very real regret'.

The legendary Frederick Jacob died in Kashmir on the 1st September of that year.

Back at Felsted the first months were spent in making good the damage to buildings and grounds inflicted by the various Army units which had succeeded one another. The Pioneer Corps had been the first occupants of the Junior House and they had caused the worst damage. The grounds had been used as a motor transport park with wooden pillars supporting camouflage netting. Mr Hornsby, a boy living in the village at the time, remembers being given a lift in a Bren gun carrier to Woodley's Garage and the barbed wire 'as high as a tennis court' which encircled the grounds.

In 1940 the Telfers had taken 80 boys to Herefordshire. They came back to Felsted with the same number. In January 1946 they handed the Junior House over to Bryan and Meg Morris and went to Elwyn's for two terms.

4

B S Morris
1946 – 1951

Bryan Morris was appointed to the Junior House by Headmaster Alistair Andrew following an interview with him at Canon ffrome Court. He and his wife Meg came from Monkton Combe Junior School and joined the Junior House staff for Autumn term 1945 before taking up his post in the New Year. In his five years he restored the Prep to its pre-war state, removed the traces of upheaval and left it to Derek and Enid Ross in 1951 as a flourishing concern.

When they first saw the Junior House at the end of 1945, Bryan Morris describes what met them,

> The house was a shambles; on several bedroom walls you could not put your hand flat on any wall without it going into a hole. All was later filled up with concrete. The grounds were knee deep in grass and elm shoots and suckers. Imagine preparing a cricket square! Apparently some Signals Regiment had used it. The new tennis courts had been used as a coal yard. Poor Andrew Telfer had much of this to cope with. I did my best to help and fix up family.
>
> We were housed in Chaffix-Cromwellian, a filthy duck pond in front and mushrooms growing in the passage to the kitchen. Full of history to me as a historian, but! It belonged to the Bursar, Harold Moller. We were there until January 1st when we moved in in a bitter NE wind and wet fog.
>
> Junior House vast front door faced due East. So began 5 very happy years....

In common with very many prep schools during the war recruiting teaching staff had been difficult, and Morris undertook a comprehensive rebuilding in that area. During the time away from Felsted there had also developed a certain 'clannishness' – many of the masters were Old Felstedians – and there was some resentment at an 'outsider' taking charge of the Junior House and resistance to the changes which he wanted to introduce. However, Morris made his mark on the school with single-minded determination. By September 1947 the entire teaching staff, with one exception was composed of assistants of his own choosing, although the actual appointments were in the hands of the Headmaster.

J H C Walker (1946-51) was appointed Senior Master and taught Classics and coached the cricket with much success. 'Johnny' Walker had been Senior Master at Monkton Combe Junior School where G S Jameson's father was Headmaster and from where Morris had come. Jameson (1947-59), who had been taught by Morris at Monkton Combe took over responsibility for Geography and Scouts. H G Waters (OF) (1946-72) came from wartime service with the RAF to teach Maths, and made an immediate impact with his highly successful coaching of rugger and athletics – about which more later in this account. J H R Churchill (1946-51) came to teach French and hockey and E W I Mason (OF) French.

Thus at the start of Autumn term 1947 there was only one survivor of the staff with whom Andrew Telfer had returned from Herefordshire, Mrs Sprott. Olaf Simpson and Martin Hooton had already gone over to the Senior School, Simpson to be Follyfield House Tutor and Hooton as Warden of the Bury. Morris introduced half days for the staff, 'to start at 10.30 am so that they could catch the "Felsted Flyer" and get to civilisation. Those were the days!'

Sporting achievement soon began to show. 'The Autumn Term was chiefly notable for a very successful rugger season, in which we won all nine matches and scored 218 points against our opponents 17. For this we were indebted to our Captain, Currie, whose speed and thrust in attack were responsible for most of the scores.'

In March 1946 Morris wrote in the Junior House Notes in the Felstedian 'we are a full House of 83 boys with some twelve Common Entrance candidates and one taking the Scholarship'. In Summer 1947 he added, 'numbers are almost 100 for the first time in its history'. Pressure was growing for more boarding accommodation.

The Vicarage, adjoining the Junior House and on the same side of the road, would be ideal for the purpose. Morris had a family connection with the Vicar and was in a good position to suggest to Alistair Andrew the idea of acquiring the property. Andrew persuaded the Governors to buy the Vicarage in exchange for No. 2 Bury Chase. The Church Commissioners, while sanctioning the exchange, refused to allow the School to name their new acquisition 'The Old Vicarage'. Andrew had been tragically killed as the result of a car crash in February 1947, and it was decided to name the house 'Andrew's' in his memory. Permits and licences held up the alterations to the building, and for the Autumn Term of 1948 the youngest 18 boarders were lodged in Ingram's Close.

Andrew's opened in January 1948. In return for providing extra space for Junior House boarders, the School insisted that the Senior School Chaplain, the Rev L S K Ford, should be master-in-charge, together with his wife and two daughters. This proved to be less than satisfactory. Derek Ross insisted that a member of the Junior School staff should be in charge at Andrew's. Geoffrey Jameson (who had married Morris's part-time secretary, part-time Matron) moved in from Enville's and members of the Junior School staff ran Andrew's from then until it was finally closed at the end of the Summer Term of 1982, when the Governors sold it to Felsted Kindergarten School.

In June 1947 Morris wrote to parents about erecting a cricket pavilion in memory of Alistair Andrew.

> . . . and we intend to put up some memorial which will ever remind the Junior House of a great Headmaster and of one who began his teaching career at the Prep.
> Realising that there is no chance of building now, my idea was to buy a good hut and to alter it (and perhaps thatch the roof) to meet the needs of and to resemble a pavilion; something simple yet dignified to remind us of one who was admired and respected by all. . . .

A year later he was able to write,

> Thanks to the interest of a local parent, a suitable building
> was found and purchased, fortunately slightly larger than was
> essential, and, by cutting off a third, sufficient wood is available
> for a verandah, lockers and, maybe, a scoring box alongside. A
> flag, flagpole and a clock have been presented by parents, all
> of which add to the amenities of an attractive and, we hope,
> useful building, and funds permitting, deck chairs, suitable trees
> and other little extras should make the pavilion worthy of such
> a memorial.

Geoffrey Jameson was given the task of putting up the pavilion, as he
was showing a talent for assembling temporary structures around the
school. 'It seemed to me that weekend after weekend and half day
after half day I was out on Follyfield putting the blasted thing up. . . .
Harold persuaded me to join a tobacco cooperative, and it was in this
pavilion that in the Autumn I hung my crop to dry. It was duly posted
off and came back after fermentation; it was revolting, neither of us could
smoke it.'

The Andrew pavilion was ready for use in the Summer Term of
1949, sited on the edge of Follyfield near the grass tennis courts.
It was in full use until the night of July 14th 1976, the year of
a very hot and dry summer, when it was completely destroyed by
fire.

Junior House magazines had appeared intermittently before, usually
on roneoed foolscap stapled between red covers. The only other news
published about the Prep was to be found in occasional 'Junior House
Notes' in the Felstedian. Morris started the Young Felstedian – 'hardly
inspiring and not very informative', he admits – edited by Geoffrey
Jameson and John Churchill (staff 1947-51) until the latter left. It was
printed by May and Brett of Dunmow.

The inaugural number reported the opening of Andrew's House for
18 boarders and the whole holiday given to the school to mark the
occasion of the Royal Wedding (Princess Elizabeth and Prince Philip).
It has appeared without a break since then, its production methods and
its purposes as a modern school magazine being far more sophisticated
now than in those earlier, more innocent days.

In 1949 the Wilson building was put up between Cloisterfield and
Rose Cottage. An engraved brass plate read,

This Hall was built in AD 1949 by the generous
bequest of
PERCEVAL RICHARD WILSON
at Felsted 1867-1874 and a Governor of the School 1930-1938

P R Wilson was also a President of the OF Society, and it had been his idea to convert one of the houses between the Chequers Inn and Elwyn's into the new Cricket Pavilion, opened in 1933. He died in February 1947, and in his will he left '... the annual gift of a bat to the best cricketer in the Junior House'. Morris recalls that the new Bursar, John Reading, had it put up as an experiment. 'The walls went up by a donkey machine, and the men had to keep the concrete pouring in .... Wilson Hall was a vital and urgent necessity, as there was nowhere else we could meet – except the Chapel – as a whole school. And the Chapel was too sacred!'

Wilson consisted of two classrooms separated by a folding wooden wall. It was put to many uses. In the days straight after the war the School Play had been put on in the 'tin gym' where Ross hall now stands. There were difficulties in constructing a stage for each year's production, and the stage and curtains were therefore moved to Wilson as a fixture, only flats and lighting being erected for the actual performance. The stage was stoutly built and, when, in Derek Ross's time, Godfrey Bullard (staff 1954-60) produced Sweeny Todd, there was great difficulty in cutting a trap door so that the corpses could fall beneath from the barber's chair.

Wilson was also used as a prep room for the whole school with one master on supervision duty each evening, as the school library, and finally as the Games Room with table tennis and snooker tables. It was demolished in Autumn 1993 to make way for the new two-storey classroom block added on to the Cloister Wing.

Scouting was pursued with great enthusiasm, boys being encouraged but not dragooned into becoming Scouts. Jameson took over a Troop of four patrols from Charles Tunks together with an enormous collection of useless cooking gear, very little kit and hardly any canvas. At first the Senior School Scoutmaster helped run the Troop, but Morris characteristically gave every encouragement to Jameson to follow an independent line. There was no Scout Hut, and to start with the gear was stored in the attic over the Headmaster's garage. Then Jameson put up a hut behind the Hobby House (now the CDT room) and, with a capitation fee from the Bursar, started to assemble equipment including pioneering gear and five 160lb ex-Army tents, one for each patrol and one for use as a store tent.

Jameson's first camp was held at Fittleworth in Sussex in the first week after the end of the Summer Term on the estate where Colonel Blacker had perfected the infantry anti-tank weapon (PIAT). It was a thrilling site for the boys with remains of armoured vehicles blown to pieces hidden in the bracken. Jameson had had nothing to do with Scouting since his own pre-school days, but his five years in the Army provided him with basic know-how, as it had indeed with Baden-Powell. Central cooking, provided by two cooks from the Junior House was replaced by patrol cooking.

Harold Waters always paid a visit of a night to two to these Summer Camps. His own hike tent was usually badly sited and pitched, he never made or hung out his bed and washed during flagbreak and prayers, but he was immensely popular. Jameson remembers, 'He took endless photos, ate the most revolting uncooked and over-burnt food without complaint, told very complicated ghost stories at campfire and never complained about the weather. In later years he sometimes made life difficult by taking athletes to White City for the day, and I would find myself without any effective patrol leaders'.

The Troop was run much on Harold Waters' lines. His rugger was backed up by endless charts showing players' skills and progress as indeed was his athletics. Every Scout had his progress card up on the wall of the hut, and each day in break the Scouter would go to teach, test and record the good news.

The Scouts needed a permanent site on which to practise their skills, and, when the School acquired the Vicarage (Andrew's), the part of the garden nearest to the Junior House became the Scout Patch, only in bounds to Scouts. Here in the Summer Term each patrol made a patrol kitchen, built gadgets and were allowed to light fires and cook on Sundays. The chances of food rather than wide games down Jollyboys lane increased the numbers to six and then to eight patrols. The Scout Patch now forms part of the Pre-Prep premises.

The tin-roofed hut behind the Hobby House soon became inadequate, and in 1955 a builder parent, Mr Barker, found an ex-wartime sectional building going cheap. Jameson and his Scouts assembled it themselves, but it was never entirely satisfactory, being without electricity, too large for a store and too small for a meeting room. It was eventually pulled down in 1985, all the equipment being disposed of some time before. Where it stood are now gardens for the children.

Summer camps continued, first North of Leith Hill and then on the Norfolk-Suffolk border. There was a patrol competition and the Patrol leader of the winning patrol received a Gilwell hand axe, his No, 2 a sheath knife. Each year the District would organise a camping competition in Hatfield Forest. The Junior House Troop went all out to win or at very least to beat the Senior School Troop. A Scout Troop continued in existence until the late 1960's at the Junior School.

In 1951 Bryan and Meg Morris returned to Monkton Combe Junior School. Morris took over the headmastership from Geoffrey Jameson's father on the latter's retirement. With him he took J H C Walker, and Harold Waters took over as Senior Master. Bryan Morris has the last word – 'We loved the challenge in a jolly fine school'.

5

The Rev D L Ross
1951 – 1971

Bryan and Meg Morris were followed at the Junior House by the Rev
Derek Ross and his wife Enid. Both men had applied for Monkton
Combe. Morris got the post, but urged Headmaster Harrison to appoint
Derek Ross.

Derek Ross had been educated at St Lawrence College, Ramsgate,
where he had been a fag of Morris and of whose Old Boys Society
he was later President. He went on to Exeter College, Oxford, where
he obtained a degree in Geography. He gained a Hockey Blue and
played for the University for three years. After training at Wycliffe Hall,
Oxford, he entered the Ministry and worked as curate of St Helen's,
Lancashire. During the war he was vicar of Altcar and then Chaplain and
Housemaster at Liverpool College. When he retired, Douglas Millard,
the Bursar and one of the Ross's many friends, wrote:

> . . . his personality has a magnetic charm, which radiates warmth and
> friendliness, and it is seasoned with a delightful sense of humour
> which is accentuated by a slight stutter. His sermons have frequently
> displayed this, and he would maintain attention often by making
> some startling announcement during the sermon. . . .

It is not surprising that his Junior School Chapel services were popular
with parents and boys alike. Enid Ross played a large part in the success

of Derek's Headship with a sense of humour which could break through in even the most frustrating situation. In the housekeeping side of the school Enid could always rely on the loyalty of her staff, some of whom stayed with her until she left.

During his 21 years as Head of the Junior School numbers rose from 101 to 140, new classrooms, the Art Room and Ross Hall were built and extra dormitories made available. It was a time of steady growth with parents, staff and boys acting closely together.

It did take the Ross's a little time to find their feet in the prep school system to begin with. In Geoffrey Jameson's words:

> . . . the term 'Prefect' to Derek meant a large and effective boy to whom you could delegate real responsibility. He was amazed at the sheer nannying which went on with small boys; though he loved sport, he was amazed at the volume of competition, the endless adding of charts, the endless requests that he congratulate someone at Saturday morning's assembly for clearing a certain height at High Jump, when clearly the child had no hope of athletic success. It was, however, not long before he came to terms with the different demands of prep school life and from then on there was no turning back.

In 1951 the staffing of the Junior School was:

The Rev D L Ross M.A. (Oxon) Master in Charge
H G Waters (OF) B.A. (Cantab)
G S Jameson   M.A. (Cantab)
C K Hills   M.A. (Cantab)
N W P Davies   M.A. (Oxon)
A H Birchall   B.A. (Oxon)
Miss B Tozer
Miss J M Reynolds

Until the end of the 1960's most, if not all, of the male staff were Oxbridge graduates. It was the custom that, on arrival at the Junior School, they should provide their College shield which would then be displayed with those of other masters, past or present, on the walls of the Dining Room. The custom has lapsed, but many of the shields still hang there.

In 1952 the annual fees were: Boarders – £261 – a composite fee; Day Boys – £90 – £75 tuition, £15 additional non-tuition fee.

In that year it was noted in the Young Felstedian that '...the wind has blown away the rooks' nests from the elm trees'. These elm trees are clearly shown in the 1875 map on page 3, running North-South as an old field boundary on the East side of Cloisterfield. Three of them remained standing, tall and massive, still with rooks' nests, until the mid-1960's, but there was a danger of falling branches and they were cut down.

During this period there were many acts of generosity by individual parents, too many to record all of them here, which greatly added to the appearance of the school or to the benefit of the boys. The parents of Robert Barker gave, in 1954, the weather vane on the roof of Telfer's West Wing. It depicts a Cromwellian ship chasing a sea serpent, and on the base there is a reproduction of the School crest.

Since his arrival at the Junior House, as it was then known, Harold Waters had been coaching athletics by patient encouragement and meticulous attention to technique in both Field and Track, aided by a multitude of photographs which he took of the boys in action, a forerunner of coaching by video film. Long hours were spent in the Summer Term, afternoons and evenings, on Cloisterfield which was provided with a running track, High Jump and Long Jump pits (the latter with a Pole Vault box) and a circle for Hammer, Discus and Shot.

From the early 1950's his efforts bore fruit with names such as Burleigh, Addis, Morris, Reynolds and Felgate featuring in the records. In 1952 Michael Burleigh's performances in all 12 scheduled events 'were quite remarkable for anybody of his size, for at the age of 13 and a half he was only 4'8" tall and weighed about 75 pounds'. All four Burleigh brothers were at the Prep and the wrought iron Burleigh gates at the entrance to the Headmaster's drive commemorate them – John, Michael, Peter and Edward. The gates were put up in 1960 and feature their names and the dates of the years they were at the Junior School.

1954 was one of the peaks of Harold Waters' coaching career. In June Stuart Morris (son of Bryan and Meg) had won the 880 in a time of 2.28.5, 'a quite remarkable time for anybody of his size and age'. And then, on the last day of his last Summer Term, Robert Addis cleared

9'9" in the Pole Vault, 'a feat that can have been beaten by very few 13 year olds anywhere'. Harold Waters pointed out that this height:

a) would have been 3rd in the first modern Olympics
b) would have been 7th best for any age group in Essex in 1954
c) had beaten the Senior School record up to July 1953; it had been at 9'0" since 1939.

Addis became AAA Junior Pole Vault Champion in 1957, and in his last Sports at the Junior School achieved Special Standards in all 12 events. This last distinction he shared with John Reynolds who was also an especially fine hurdler. Another athlete whom Waters started on the road to athletic distinction was shot putter Martyn Lucking who left the Prep in 1951. Two years later, aged 15, he held the Felsted record and a year after leaving school represented Great Britain against Poland and East Germany. He competed in the 1960 Rome Olympics and again in 1964 and took part in the Commonwealth Games of 1958, 1962 (where he won a Gold Medal) and 1970.

A new dormitory was completed over the Library at the end of the Cloister wing and named Morris after Derek Ross's predecessor. This and the adjacent large Canon ffrome dormitory were closed in 1992, because of the shrinkage in boarding numbers, and were converted into a flat for the Resident Assistant Master and his wife. Also in 1954 a domestic servants room in the oldest part of the building was changed to dormitory use. Numbers were on the increase!

Scouting and Cubs continued to play a large part in school life with rafting and bridging on the Chelmer, preparing campsites on the Scout Patch, cooking, attending Rallies and Summer Camps being tackled with the greatest enthusiasm. As mentioned earlier, under the direction of their Scoutmaster, Geoffrey Jameson, the Scouts assembled in 1955 their Scout Hut. Scouting, but not Cubs, continued into the late 60's. A favourite pastime was descending the aerial ropeway which started from the top of the beech tree in the corner of the Scout Patch (now included in the Pre-Prep site). It came to an end at a sturdy tripod at the opposite corner. Lighter boys made a leisurely journey down to the tripod, the heavyweights landed with a bump on the poles.

It was finally decided in 1968 that Patrick Higgins, who had taken over the Scouts with one helper, could not run a Troop of 48 Scouts in such a way as to accomplish all the activities and testing for qualifications which were required by the Scout Movement. Rather than reduce the number of boys taking part, it was thought better to withdraw from Scouting yet try to carry on much as before. The Scouts were now called Rangers. They continued with the same type of activity, including Monday afternoons, a weekend camp in the Summer Term and a Summer Camp in the long holidays. The two camps no longer take place, but a Leavers' Camp after the Common Entrance Exams fulfils much the same purpose. The demolition of the Scout Hut in 1985 and the dispersal of the remaining equipment saw the end of the chapter.

By 1956 numbers had reached 120, the great majority of whom were still boarders. The three-mile rule for day boys was still observed. The school continued to change for games in the old green-painted corrugated iron 'gym' built in 1909 for 40 boys, and they would continue to do so for another fourteen years.

The Autumn number of the Young Felstedian recorded the third name by which the Prep was to be known. '...at the *Junior School*, please note that change of name.' No longer, officially, was it the Junior House.

In the same year the Dining Hall was panelled with oak, and 'it certainly has more dignity when the room is empty, though it is to be doubted whether the manners of some of us can ever be made more impressive even with oak.' Plus ça change! The panelling of the Dining Hall was such a success that it was followed up next year by similar additions in the front hall and along the passage to the Headmaster's study. This further panelling was the gift of parents, the Wilkinsons, the Bakers and the Collinsons.

In June 1957 the Junior School went 'across the road' to see the first Royal visit, by Princess Alexandra. 'A black, shiny car came through the entrance with a policeman on a motorcycle at the head. Everybody cheered and clapped as she got out and shook hands. Then all the Junior School boys walked back talking excitedly....' Much the same was to happen when the Princess Royal opened the Lord Riche Hall thirty two years later except that the shiny, black car was now a red helicopter.

September 1959 was marked by a change in the form system. Until then boys moved up the school form by form, spending one, two or three terms in each form according to their ability. Now they were to be divided into two streams, A and B, and would remain in each form for a year at a time. There was as yet no separate Scholarship form. Form V contained the Scholarship candidates, plus any boys who had completed a year in IVA without taking Common Entrance. Outflow from the top end of the school was dictated by the vacancies which occurred termly in the Senior School. There were now 133 boys in the school, and it is interesting to note that 22 of these were sons of OF's. Boarding fees were now £285 pa.

On June 28th 1959 the Junior School Morning Service was televised on ATV. 'Everything went extremely well, and it was fitting that, for many hundreds of viewers, their first introduction to Felsted should have been through its Chapel'. (*Report in the Felstedian.*)

Access to the Quad from the main road had been by way of a dilapidated fence behind which was an ugly and muddy area. In its place 'we now have two beautifully built brick walls and a wrought iron railing. We also have two neat beds which are shortly to be planted with a specially planned scheme of flowering shrubs.' This entrance was the gift of Mr and Mrs Chandler in memory of their son, Peter, who had died tragically a year before. (Peter Chandler had a brother, Paul, who went on to the Senior School.) This is the entrance to the Quad which is still used every day by the Prep School children.

Patrick Higgins joined the Staff in 1961 as Senior English Master. Shortly before he left he wrote this account of life at the Junior School as it was when he first arrived:

17 YEARS AGO
by P F Higgins

The numbers in the School have changed surprisingly little. There were ten members of staff as opposed to the present twelve, and about 130 boys, all but four boarders. There were five leagues as at present, both the duties and the powers of league captains being greater than they are today. The punishment system revolved around plus and minus points. Members of staff alone could award such things. For heinous crimes, bullying being top of the list, -8 could be awarded, which resulted in an automatic visit to the Headmaster where the -8 was wiped out by summary execution. A far more tiresome punishment was -7 twice. The culprit could only erase this blot by performing useful tasks about the school at the rate of 15 minutes per plus point. The school was a clean and tidy place, there never being any shortage of miscreant labour to pick up litter, or weed the paving stones with knives gleaned from the Scout Hut. Bread was an orderly affair conducted in almost total silence and with no delay, the usual penalty for talking being -4 = 1 hour's useful labour. Masters' ingenuity was often strained to breaking point in an effort to devise a sufficiency of jobs. Even so, a capable league captain seldom suffered more than one or two members with a minus total at the end of the week.

Classroom accommodation was pinched, forms remaining in situ, staff hurrying from lesson to lesson while the Form Captain endeavoured to maintain a minute or two of peace and order. The Vth Form, an elite, luxuriated in the comfort of what now is Reekie; IVA, IVB, IIIA occupied the remainder of the Cloister Block, IIIB the French Room, while IIA yawned in the gaping void of what is now the Wilson Building. The master presided from his throne on the stage, Wilson then performing a variety of functions. The whole school assembled there for letter writing, prep, lectures, film shows and entertainments – plays put on by the different leagues after the Christmas Feast. There was also an annual production, the AV Room – the then Library – being used as a green room. Lighting was minimal and the curtain had a way of jamming at key points in the action.

The whole school lunched simultaneously in the present dining room, seated by leagues in order of seniority, and Mr Ross, the then Headmaster, encouraged boys to have at least three topics of conversation each lunch time with which to regale the members of staff next to whom they sat. One boy, unusually taciturn, spent a whole week without passing a single word. Lunch was a formal affair, being borne on vast platters from the kitchen by uniformed staff. All stood for grace at the start and end of the meal, which lasted from 1 to 1.30, at which time boys filed directly up to Rest. Table napkins were passed in wicker baskets down the table, each boy spotting and extracting his own. When noise reached too high a level (there might be some delay in the kitchen though this was surprisingly rare), Mr Ross would bang with his gavel for a few minutes' total silence.

Nothing would be heard but muted munching, while masters glared discouragingly down the ranks of their table. Telfer (now the Office) acted as an overflow room for those the dining room could not accommodate.

The present changing rooms were day rooms. The Staff Room was where stationery is now given out. The Staff Room, (now part of the entrance lobby where notices are displayed), was part day room, part tuck and stationery store. A key room in the school was the 'gym', a corrugated iron structure with wooden floor and walls, erected in 1909 as a temporary measure. It survived over 40 years, boys sitting by leagues on fixed wooden benches around its perimeter. Its dilapidation was such that practically no activity could injure it further. In winter, British bulldogs was a favourite pastime while the old iron stove glowed red. Iron railings protected boys from incineration, though it was reputed that sadistic Seniors roasted unfortunate 'nips' whose conduct had displeased them.

In addition to being the general assembly point, the gym housed tuck boxes containing the owners' wordly belongings, while on pegs above hung games clothes, caps and macintoshes. Not only was the gym the most dilapidated building in the School, it was also the one most used.

Academically the main difference was that all subjects counted towards C.E. There were two Latin papers, two Maths, but only one English, essay and comprehension being combined in one. Other subjects, though far more academic in content, were as at present with one notable exception – the only Science taught in the School (and that by myself!) was in the first form. It was known as Nature Study and ranged from astronomy to birds and bees. It was certainly fun for the teacher. Art was soon to blossom as a major force, while music within 5 years was to see over half the school playing musical instruments. One concert, performing a work specially composed by the Music Master, featured an orchestra of fifty boys, the only adult being the conductor.

Finally to games. They were as at present and the standard in all was high. The 1st XV had for many seasons been unbeaten, both hockey and cricket were strong (the 1960 hockey captain went on to Captain England). 'Tours' had yet to make their appearance so the opposition was local and probably less exacting than today. Athletics was amongst the best in the country and Sports Day was the occasion of the year. The pole vault record was only a little below that of the Oxbridge Sports, a remarkable achievement, the result of long hours of devoted practice.

The 1960s saw what Mr Reekie described at one Speech Day as an 'embarrassing' increase in numbers both in the Senior and Junior Schools. In the Junior School pressure for more teaching space was badly needed. In 1962 a new classroom block on the West side of the Cloisterfield was completed and opened by Kenneth Kendall OF, the TV newsreader. He was also to open the new open air swimming pool eleven years later. Derek Ross wrote, 'Owing to the great generosity of parents (the Friends of Felsted) we were able to build four new classrooms, so that all our forms are now grouped together.' T R Foster of IVA described the scene:

> The new classroom block was ceremonially opened by Kenneth Kendall with a pair of nail scissors which he had somehow mislaid in a ventilator shaft sometime in the 1930s, while he was a member of the school. This heirloom was discovered by Robin Wakelin while hunting for his tuckbox keys.
>
> He presented them to the TV star on a velvet cushion. There was another presentation made by R O Foster, the architect, of a manicure set in a leather case, marked in gold lettering – Kenneth Kendall, July 15th 1962. After three brief speeches, Mr Kendall cut a gorgeous red and white ribbon with his newly found scissors.

These four new classrooms freed space, which had been used as Day Rooms, for new changing rooms and a Common Room for the Staff. In Tim Andrews' time these changing rooms became the Library and in 1993 the girls' changing rooms.

Work on enlarging the School Chapel started in the same year. While work was going on, the Junior School services were held in the Congregational (later United Reformed) Chapel across the road, while the Senior School used the Grignon Hall or the Parish Church. This arrangement lasted until the School Chapel was reopened in the Summer Term of 1964.

Among the many gifts which parents continued to make to the school was a ship's bell donated by Commander and Mrs Drake. It is still in daily use, rung by means of a cord on the main staircase leading to the dormitories.

The 1964 Four Hundredth Anniversary Celebrations reached their climax with the enactment of 'A Felsted Chronicle', a historical pageant produced by Alan and Marion Ronaldson. The whole school, Senior and Junior, was involved in the production. Michael Craze writes, 'to Rosemary Trew, (Junior School Art Mistress) who wrote the text of the Chronicle from my "History" the greatest credit should go'. All the music was composed by William Eden, Music Master at the Junior School. As Derek Ross wrote, 'the Mr Eden–Miss Trew formation quickly became famous'.

'A Felsted Chronicle' received widespread and enthusiastic coverage in the Press both local and national. An extract from the Essex Weekly News, similar to many others, read,

> In a production of this nature, however, the producers' burden is particularly onerous, and I know that Alan and Marion Ronaldson jointly accepted the task with grave misgivings.
>
> The result was a triumph not only technically but imaginatively, and to them must go the biggest share of praise for an evening of supreme merit and enjoyment.
>
> Their most brilliant and telling stroke of imagination came right at the end of the Chronicle.
>
> Representatives of the Felsted School of 1964, together with the full cast, were assembled in the arena. We in the audience expected the Chronicle would come to an end with them all singing 'The Queen'. Instead, they moved off, the school corps band bringing up the rear, until the arena was empty save for one small, red-capped and blazered boy.
>
> He represented 'the blood of Felsted's life, just one of those who passed through the school, continually alike, perpetually unique', a direct spiritual descendant of the first Felsted scholar who opened the Chronicle's tale.
>
> The summons of the school bell made him run over, pick up his books and start to scamper off, before he was checked by the voice of a reader proclaiming: 'Boy, the future lies with you'.
>
> Only half comprehending and more concerned with not being late for class, the boy half turned, shrugged his shoulders with an eloquence more expressive than words and ran off, thus bringing the Chronicle's time span round to its full circle.

There were 22 episodes and as well as providing the small boy at the end, the Junior School enacted 'Episode 16 – 1895; A Sunday Morning'. It was directed by Arthur Birchall, and the cast list is reproduced below

16   1895   A SUNDAY MORNING

Urchins	G Perry, D R Ross
Clergyman	Mr M Griffin
Coachman	Mr J Gates
New Woman	Miss B Atkins
Schoolboys	J R Talbot, D J Sutherland, R I S Mackay, A M Stewart, R P Handley, R H Grimshaw, F R Dannatt, A J Arden
Relations	Miss B Tozer, Mr J Packett, Miss D Edmonds,

1942

13 At Canon ffrome Court 1942. Headmaster Bickersteth is in the centre seated between the Telfers. The teaching staff to Mr Telfer's left are O I Simpson, G Thorne and Miss Fielding. To Mrs Telfer's right are M C G Hooton, R J van Leuvan, Major Sparrow and Mr Rimmer.

14 B S Morris.

15 Harold Waters with the 1949 Rugger Squad.

16 The Andrew Pavilion, built in 1948 and destroyed by fire in 1976. Photograph taken during a Fathers' match in the 1950s.

17 Scouts on Cloisterfield with the Wilson building behind. The classroom blocks beyond have yet to be built.

18 Taken between 1945 and 1947. There are no buildings between the end of Telfer's wing and the Vicarage (later Andrew's).

19 'Rest' at Camp with G S Jameson reading to the boys. One of the ex-Army tents is behind.

20 B S Morris (5th from right) at Trinity College, Cambridge with all those who had served on his staff at either Felsted or Monkton Combe, and had become I.A.P.S. Headmasters themselves. Those at Felsted were C K Hills (1949–53), far right J H R Churchill (1947–51), 2nd from right G B Stanley (Felsted 1953–59, then M.C.), 4th from right G S Jameson.

21 Derek Ross, taken in 1959.

22 The Burleigh Gates. Put up in 1960 to commemorate the four brothers, John, Michael, Peter and Edward.

23 Stuart Morris breaking the
    880-yard record, June 1954.

24 Robert Addis with the
    Pole Vault bar set at his
    record-breaking height of
    9ft 9ins, July 1954.

25 Plate racing at one of the earlier camps, about 1950.

26 The store tent. Leaning against the tent pole is J Reynolds. Next to him is S Wilkes. Scoutmaster Jameson is cutting up a large can of bully beef. Summer 1950.

27 The Dining Hall in 1959. League tables are set for a meal. The George and Dragon trophy is on the wall next to the doors. The new oak panelling can be seen.

28 July 14th, 1962. Robin Wakelin, Kenneth Kendall OF, Mr and Mrs Telfer, D.L.R.

29 "Boy, the future lies with you".

30 Derek and Enid Ross on their retirement in 1971.

31 Oliver and Pauline Pemberton, 1978.

32 Typical of the photographs which Harold Waters used in his Rugger coaching.

33 Helpers on Sports Day with 'Heavy Haulage' and 'Little Pram'. Behind them is Church House.

34 Harold Waters in his retirement year, 1972.

35 One half of the swimming pool backing down the drive.

36 Kenneth Kendall OF starting the inaugural relay race. Gaselee in the picture, Jeremy Bright, League Captain, last to race. May 1973.

37 The newly completed Hunnable Hobby House. Summer 1974.

38 Tim and Chrissi Andrews.

39 Glazing of Cloisters completed, 1981. Paving slabs on the "Downs" were to be replaced with bricks in 1985. The flowering cherry was removed at the same time.

40 Humphrey and Denise Watts, Summer 1979.

41 The new changing rooms under construction . . .

42 . . . and completed, 1983.

43 & 44 Bricking the 'Downs', 1985.

	Mr H Eden, Mrs H Eden, Mr A Birchall, Miss S Millar, Mr M Wallington, Mrs B Wotherspoon, Miss E Davey, Miss S Page, Miss C Halliday, J P M Nicholls, M K Suggett, J G Wheatley
Nurse	Miss R Trew

Somewhat overshadowed by the excitement of the celebrations was the building of a second block of three classrooms close to the 'Crittall' block of four completed two years before. The final extension of teaching facilities by Derek Ross was the new Art Room built in 1968 with funds provided from the same Appeal which gave the Junior School the Ross Hall. Having an Art Room on the premises saved the daily trek to the 'Rabbit Hutch', the building behind Ingram's Close which is now used for the Senior School's 6th Form Club.

The final and major event which came at the end of Derek Ross's Headship was the building of the Ross Hall. It was opened on the 1st October 1970 by Lord Butler of Saffron Walden and was the result of an Appeal which within nine months raised £45,000, most of it contributed by Parents and Old Boys. The balance left over went to provide a Junior School Science laboratory at the main school for teaching the Nuffield Science course. The laboratory has since been absorbed into the Senior School facilities and Science is taught on the Prep School premises. The architect was again R O Foster, an OF and old Junior School parent.

The new Hall replaced the old 'gym' which has featured from time to time in this account. Derek Ross wrote:

> Our old Gym started to come down at the end of the term in December 1969. It was rather a nostalgic moment. It took some time for all the building to be demolished. Underneath the floorboards were found 23 table tennis balls, a carton for a Lyons Fruit Pie (price 2d.) and also a History exercise book belonging to a boy who left in 1927. The boys saw a big change after the Easter holidays as the walls were up and the concrete roof beams in place. They missed the excitement in the holidays of seeing the large crane moving the beams into position. . . . We trust that it will be in full operation by the beginning of the September Term. (It was!)

Derek Ross was always proud of the later success of boys who had passed through his hands. Mention should be made of two of them who achieved distinction in the same sport at which he had shone at Oxford. One was Richard Oliver (fa 1953-63). He captained the English Public Schools Hockey team and played for the Essex County XI while still at school. He went on to captain Oxford, played for England and competed in the 1968 and 1972 Olympic Games. The other was Robert Cattrall (fh 1966-75). From Felsted he went on to play hockey for Wales and Great Britain and won a Bronze Medal in the 1984 Olympic Games.

Already showing signs of his future academic eminence at the Junior School and at Felsted, where he was a Scholar, was Robin Briggs (fg 1950-60). He went on to become Senior Research Fellow at All Souls College, Oxford, specialising in Modern French History.

Another source of pride was the fact that so many of his Staff went from the Junior School to become Headmasters of other Schools. They included G S Jameson, G B Stanley, M R Smith, M W Kelham and A H Birchall.

On leaving Felsted, after a very rewarding twenty one years, Derek and Enid Ross took the living of Stebbing and finally retired to Brighton.

6

O J B Pemberton
1971 – 1978

Oliver Pemberton came to Felsted with considerable experience of teaching at prep schools, having been a master at King's College School, Cambridge and Clifton Junior School and Headmaster of Pownall Hall School, Cheshire. He was a versatile games player – he coached the 1st XI Hockey for four years – and an enthusiastic and successful producer of plays. He was aware that the days were numbered of the traditional, old-fashioned prep school; changing social attitudes and a harsher economic climate meant that schools would have to compete to be successful.

Soon after his appointment his wife, Elizabeth, died tragically in a car accident. He offered to withdraw, but the Governors pressed him to continue, which he did. To support him in running the domestic and secretarial sides of the school he enlisted the help of Miss Pauline Venables. They married during the Christmas holidays of 1973/74.

One of the first things which Pemberton did was to involve parents more closely with the teaching staff by initiating parents' meetings, form by form, to discuss the academic progress of their sons. This was followed by other, more social activities, which brought parents more closely into the school's life. This was further developed by Tim Andrews who gave it the name 'Partnership'.

In 1972 Harold Waters retired. Mention has been made of his

contribution to the Junior School before in this account. An Old Felstedian, H G Waters was appointed by Bryan Morris in 1946 after war service in the RAF as a Navigator. He taught only Mathematics and took a special pride in producing top class mathematicians. He was an inspired Rugger coach with a fine record of wins. His long and detailed match reports, in which individual and team performances were analysed, always had clusters of boys studying them. Harold could frequently be seen standing at the foot of the main staircase after the boys' Tea, holding his pipe in his hand and talking over tactics on the Duty Master's board.

Harold Waters was also, as mentioned before, an outstanding Athletics coach, and spent hours of his spare time in the Summer evenings on Cloisterfield encouraging and teaching the boys the finer points of Track and Field. He also enthused non-athletes into providing a back-up service where each boy had his specific job. One of the most coveted was to be in charge of an old pram named 'Heavy Haulage' which was laden with stop watches, tape measures and markers and wheeled from event to event. On the ditch side of Cloisterfield was an open-sided shelter called 'Church House' after the parents who had donated it. From there Harold Waters organised activities and kept the pole vault poles, high jumps and the rakes and shovels for the sand pits. During the Summer term the corridor leading to Ross Hall was lined with multi-coloured charts showing individual achievements in the greatest detail and always meticulously updated.

After school hours Harold would go to relax in the Chequers sitting on his favourite stool in a corner of the bar. He had a warm relationship with Joe Ripton, the landlord, who had flown Catalina flying boats during the war. Both men had trained at bases in Canada and the United States at the same time. To Joe Ripton's wife Mac he brought herrings and sprats from Mersea where he lived after moving from the Norfolk Broads. At Mersea he kept a boat, and in the Ripton's garage at Felsted a vintage car, a chain-driven Frazer-Nash.

Harold Waters died in 1982, leaving in his Will a provision that the boys of the Junior School should continue to enjoy a Strawberry and Cream tea at his expense every Summer term. His Will also provided funds for enlarging the 'lobby' inside the Red Doors, the front entrance to the school from the Quad.

The building of the classroom blocks, the Art Room and the new Hall in Derek Ross's last years had been the main structural developments since the Telfers' extensions of 1934. The next five years saw the completion of further major projects which changed the appearance of the school.

The first of these, in 1973, was a 40 foot outdoor heated swimming pool. The site chosen was the Headmaster's private garden at the far end of the grounds between Follyfield and Cloisterfield, for long a place of relaxation which was out of bounds to the boys and guarded with beech hedges. The garden comprised a lawn, flower beds and vegetable garden. From its inception the Prep had used the indoor Swimming Pool at the Senior School, and the time was now considered ripe for it to have its own separate facility.

The Friends of Felsted financed the scheme and many parents gave additional support. Mr Regan, Managing Director of Globe Construction Company, who had a son at the Junior School, offered to build the pool at reduced cost. Work started at the start of the Summer term. A large pit was excavated and the spoil was heaped on top of the old vegetable beds next to the boundary ditch. The two halves of the fibre glass pool were brought down the drive past the Headmaster's house on low loaders, lifted on to girders over the pit, and bolted together. The completed shell was then lowered in, the pump house and filtration connected and the pool filled with 30,000 gallons of water. A 4-inch pipe had to be borrowed from the Harlow Fire Brigade to bring the water the 250 yards from the hydrant outside the school gates. The whole operation was completed in five days, from May 1st – 5th. On a cold, wet Saturday morning Oliver Pemberton and Mr Regan unofficially opened the pool by diving in in front of the assembled boys.

The official opening took place on the 19th May. The guest of honour was Kenneth Kendall, who had opened a new classroom block in 1962. He started the inaugural League relay race in which fifty boys took part, while the rest of the school cheered them on in the steady rain as if it had been a Cup Final. Three years later, changing rooms became available when the new cricket pavilion was built. Solar panels were installed on the pavilion roof in 1982 as a back-up for the oil-fired heating.

In the Summer of 1974 two more projects were completed. Along the path to Andrew's beyond the Scout Hut (demolished in 1985) was built the 'Hunnable Hobby House', named after Mr T F Hunnable, who provided the funding and whose three sons, Martyn, Christopher and Julian, were all at the Junior School. Thomas Hunnable became a Governor until his untimely death in 1985. He always took the closest interest in the Junior School, and he and his wife, Edna, were always sure of a warm welcome on their frequent visits. The Hobby House, his help in building the new pavilion and providing a hut for the newly formed Pet Club were all marks of his generosity. The Hunnables also opened the grounds of their house 'Alcotes' at Bocking for the weekend camps in the Summer term and provided transport for the longer holiday camps.

It soon became evident that such a large building could be put to more effective use, and in 1980 it was divided into two. The larger part became the Science Laboratory, and Science classes no longer had to make the time-wasting journey to the Laboratory in the Senior School, especially built in 1970 for the Junior School. The other part became the French room presided over by Mr J T Packett.

The second important development of 1974 was the building of an L-shaped block of classrooms behind the 'Crittall' block. The four rooms which it provided enabled a change to be made from form rooms to subject rooms. It was now the boys who moved at the end of each lesson, not the Staff. It also released the Cloister classrooms for use as dayrooms. In 1992 this block was refurbished and together with an additional room was made available for the new Pre-Prep. At the same time the Wilson building was converted into the Library by Mrs Jones and former Library at the end of the Cloister Wing into an AV room. Mrs Marion Jones was the wife of Mr Dewi Jones who had run Felsted County Primary School with outstanding success. On his retirement Marion Jones came to the Junior School to teach the junior forms. Her expertise and enthusiasm ensured the successful transformation of Wilson which for some time had had no clearly defined purpose.

In November the School waited apprehensively for its Inspection by

H M Inspectors. To everyone's relief the Inspectors were favourably impressed by both the teaching and domestic sides of the school.

After all the activity of the previous year, it was not suprising that 1975 resumed a more normal pace. Towards the end of the Spring term Mrs Mollie Millard, wife of the Bursar, set in motion a sponsored walk in aid of the Essex Physically Handicapped Association. Soon after returning from the Easter holidays, the boys went down to the old Felsted railway station and set off along the old abandoned track to Takeley. This was still possible, for the Dunmow bypass had not yet been made. One of the boys who went on the walk wrote afterwards:

> There and back is just about 21 miles. On the banks were cowslips and primroses, and we passed a wood full of bluebells. The trail was often waterlogged and muddy and covered with cinders and slaggy chips, not ideal for a long hike. After 5 miles well needed refreshments were provided by Mr Tozer and Mr Higgins looked after sore feet with a 'blister service'. With 10 miles gone the fatter and more blistered began to drop out. In all just under 50 boys completed the walk, a third of the school. Cheques totalling over £1,200 have been sent to EPHA.

The end of the Summer term was notable for the Grand Summer Fete part of a Festival of Felsted in aid of the Friends of Felsted, and also for the presence of Sir Geoffrey Howe, at Speech Day.

Brian Lippitt, who was the first Science master proper at the Junior School and took over the Rugger from Harold Waters, moved to Wolverhampton in 1975. His place in both these duties was taken by M J Higham, who became Senior Master on the retirement of J T Packett in 1987.

The impending recession had not yet affected numbers at either Junior or Senior Schools; indeed pressure on places was higher than ever. However, the trend away from boarding had started to gather pace. At a special meeting of the Governors in 1973 future policy on the increasing pressure for dayboy places was discussed. A feeling emerged strongly that Felsted was primarily a boarding school and that dayboy places should be limited. A maximum of 45 was to be the quota for the Junior School. The numbers for that year were:-

	Senior School	*Junior School*
Boarding	420	113
Day	18	34
Girls	22	–
Total	460	147

This gave a grand total of 607 pupils, the first time numbers had topped 600. But the writing was on the wall. Despite a record 154 boys at the Junior School, there were, in 1975, 106 boarders and 48 dayboys. This trend continued, caused by changing attitudes to boarding and to the worsening economic climate.

1976 will be remembered as the year of the Great Drought. By mid-Summer the grass on the playing fields had dried to a yellow-brown colour and a mosaic of deep cracks had appeared. Early in the holidays, on the night of July 13th/14th, a fire started in the Andrew Pavilion. Fanned by a strong breeze, it soon reduced the wooden building and all the sports equipment stowed in it to a low mound of ash and charred timbers. Only the cricket scoreboard with the figures for the last match was left standing to one side of the ruin.

Planning permission was eventually given to erect a new pavilion on the corner of Follyfield next to the Swimming Pool. Mr Thomas Hunnable provided a temporary pavilion for the 1977 cricket season and supplied at cost the 'Spectraglaze' blocks for building the walls.

1977 was the year of the Queen's Silver Jubilee, and, in commemoration, a programme of treeplanting was started in the Spring. Twenty one trees were planted as well as several yards or hedging, beeches along the drive and evergreens as shelter around the Swimming Pool. The most visible trees today are the five poplars behind the Design and Technology room.

During the Summer term the Junior School enjoyed an experience which is unlikely to be repeated. Four Headmasters past and present preached on separate Sundays in Chapel. They were the Rev A C Telfer, Mr B S Morris, the Rev D L Ross and Mr O J B Pemberton.

A feature of Oliver Pemberton's time at the Junior School was the series of light-hearted entertainments which he produced, some of which were set to music. In his first year 'A Ballad of King Arthur' was presented by Paddy Millard (book) and Roger Lawrence (music).

Then followed 'Androcles and the Lion' in 1973, 'Toad of Toad Hall' in 1974, 'Tom Sawyer' in 1975, 'Captain Scuttleboom's Treasure' in 1976 and 'The Thwarting of Baron Bolligrew' in 1977. At the end of his last Summer term (previous plays had been put on in March) he produced 'Let's Make an Opera' by Eric Crozier and Benjamin Britten with a mixed cast of Staff and boys as part of the Festival of Felsted.

After the Christmas Feast one year the boys were seated, expecting the usual film, when the Ross Hall stage curtains were opened, and to their great suprise and delight the Staff performed an entertainment entitled 'Babes in the Wood'. Oliver Pemberton had written it in rhyming couplets so that the lines could be learnt with the minimum rehearsal at the end of a busy term.

Robert Barsby's time as Master in charge of the Junior School Music and Chapel Choir (he was still responsible to the Director of Music at the Senior School) coincided exactly with the seven years of Pemberton. Under his direction Choral and Instrumental music flourished. In 1972 four boys were chosen to play in the IAPS Orchestra at the start of the Summer holidays. They were Nigel Watts (violin), Andrew Langton and Mark Stephenson ('cellos) and Stephen Church (trombone).

At the end of the Summer term 1973 there was a performance of 'Noye's Fludde' in the School Chapel in which nearly every boy in the school took part.

> The evening passed off very well. The orchestra, conducted by Robert Barsby, made many spendid sounds ... the singing was often stirring, the set was simply effective – I liked the palm tree – all the costumes looked good and the animal masks (much hard work put in by Gillian Cresswell, the J S Art mistress), both held and worn, quite superbly drawn ... the Voice of God speaks throughout in sonorous declamation and Mr J T Packett was awe-inspiring. But the real joy to me lay in the performance of the six solo children, Noye's sons and daughters-in-law, who have some exciting diatonic music to sing. They attacked all their numbers with tremendous glee and vigour and some fine singing. The solo voices were those of Colin Perkins, Martin Eldred, Guy Stephenson, Ian Yeldham, Paul Shadbolt and, perhaps especially Andrew Langton. (*From a report in the Felstedian*)

The Choir trip to York Minster in 1976 was especially memorable and included three Evensongs, a Recital and a performance of Faure's

Requiem. The party travelled North in Mr Thomas Hunnable's luxurious horsebox. Robert Barsby wrote about the return journey to Felsted,

> . . . and I'll bet it's the first time that Byrd's Ave Verum had been heard issuing from a horsebox on the southbound carriageway of the A1, note perfect, and from memory too.

The visit to York was followed next year by one to Canterbury in April. 'No one will every forget the Sung Eucharist on Sunday morning. One had a great feeling of pilgrimage and of being at the centre of the Anglican Church.' In July the Choir sang at the Britten and Bernstein Concert at the South Weald Festival and then at the Felsted Festival. The work by Leonard Bernstein was the Chichester Psalms, sung in Hebrew. Of the performance a music critic wrote,

> The effect was electric and memorable. Mr Barsby commanded his forces with a sure touch, and the Basses and Tenors who co-operated were as smooth and mellow as the excellently trained boys.

Robert Barsby's last contribution to Junior School music was at the end of Summer term 1978 when he organised the music for the production of 'Let's Make an Opera'. He left Felsted to become Director of Music at Pangbourne.

On the sporting scene the four Stephenson brothers, Mark, Guy, Paul and John stood out in all three major games, and especially in cricket. Of John Stephenson the master in charge of the 1st XI, J R 'Bob' Tozer remarked at the end of the 1978 season:

> J P Stephenson; A young player of great promise. His record will be hard to beat. He plays very straight and times the ball beautifully. He gets plenty of body into his bowling and has a beautiful pair of hands. He captained a happy side with increasing confidence and imagination. Well done!

He went on to play for Felsted School, Essex and England. At the end of that year Mr Pat Stephenson, their father, presented a Cup to be contested at the annual Fathers' Match in celebration of his ten years as a Father of Junior School boys.

Miss Betty Tozer, who joined the Staff in 1951, retired from full-time teaching in 1978, but went to Andrew's as Housemistress until the School sold the building. Her main area of teaching was Junior Mathematics, but her influence extended to many other areas. She ran 'stationery' from the old Common Room (now incorporated in to the entrance hall), and former J.S. boys will remember her insistence that every line in an exercise book had to be filled before a new one was issued. She also encouraged the boys with their gardens and coached the Colts hockey and cricket. As Derek Ross wrote in appreciation,

> . . . she always demanded the highest standard whether for herself or for the boys. She did not approve of slackness or slipshod work, and, though there may at times have been some who found it initially irksome, they came most certainly to appreciate her and all that she stood for. . . . She always demanded good manners, whether at table or in general dealings in the School....

In the same year Patrick Higgins left after 17 years at the Junior School. Trained as a Barrister, he brought to his teaching of English a care for ordered thinking and the well chosen word. His experience of mountaineering and ski-ing gave authority to his organisation of the Scouts, later Rangers, and with the annual ski-ing expeditions. He moved from Felsted with his wife Sally and son Jason to Woodcote House School in Surrey.

After 20 years as a prep school Headmaster, including seven years at the Junior School, Oliver Pemberton decided to give more of his time to teaching, and left Felsted to become Director of Studies at Arnold Lodge School in Warwickshire.

7

T M Andrews
1978 – 1991

Tim Andrews, his wife Chrissi and young son William arrived from Witham School, near Bourne in Lincolnshire. He soon made a mark with his extrovert personality and the cheerful approach, spiced with an element of showmanship, with which he involved himself in all school activities. He sang Tenor in the Choir and accompanied them on all their trips both at home and abroad, establishing notably a strong connection with Aachen. He also took part in the sporting tours, Leavers' Camps and the annual Canal Trips. His forté was the production of the Summer Term plays, which were now designed to fit in with Festivals of Felsted and to be the climax of the school's activities for the year. He believed in close association with parents, which he termed 'Partnership', and ensured that the Prep School was kept in the public eye through Open Days and regular releases to the local press.

Retirement and career moves meant a larger than usual number of Staff changes in 1978. Christopher Fitzgerald took over English from Patrick Higgins and became Senior Resident Master in charge of the boarders. Mrs Val Chater (OF) succeeded Gillian Cresswell as Art Mistress and Dawn Foster, who was to marry Simon Tibbitts (OF) in 1983, took over Junior Maths from Miss B Tozer. Bryan Gipps filled the post left by Robert Barsby as Master in Charge of the Junior School Choir and Music. Unchanged from the Pemberton time were:

J T Packett	Senior Master and French
D J Armour	History
H R Watts	Geography
M J Higham	Science
D J Slater	Classics
J R Tozer	Mathematics
G J Garrett	
Mrs G M Wyatt	Junior Forms

The first concern of Tim Andrews on taking over the Junior School was to improve the rather Spartan conditions in which the boarders lived, especially necessary in view of the changing attitudes now making themselves felt. In the first two years all the dormitories and most of the corridors were fitted with curtains, and a rolling programme of carpet-tiling the floors upstairs was begun. Work was started on modernising the wash-ups which still survived in their pre-war state. A laundry room was installed near the Cloth Room to cut down on the expense of outside contracting.

The most visible change outside was the enclosing and glazing of Andrew Telfer's Cloisters. The former classrooms on the ground floor, now dayrooms, were particularly vulnerable to cold and wind in the winter and waste of heat through the doors. By turning the Cloisters into an enclosed but well-lit passage, the dayrooms became an integral part of the main building. The old Headmaster's Coach House, with its adjacent 'grey area' where rubbish was incinerated. was tidied up and a garage built at the end of it.

Humphrey Watts retired at the end of the 1979 Summer Term after 13 years at the Junior School, where he taught Geography and coached Rugger and Cricket. From a schoolmastering family he came to Felsted by way of St Bees where he had taught after wartime service. Calm, shrewd and with a keen sense of humour, he and his wife Denise ran Andrew's for nearly ten years.

1980 saw the departure of two members of the domestic staff whose service stretched way back into the Ross era. They were Mrs Olive Byford and Mr Alan Raymond. A man of imposing stature – he was 6'4" tall and weighed over 15 stones – and great deliberation of movement, Alan Raymond made perceptive comments on boys whom he watched as he moved around the school. 'Being part of the furniture', as he said, the boys acted more naturally than they would have done in the presence of the teaching staff.

As mentioned in the previous section, 1980 saw the housing of the Science laboratory in one half of the Hunnable building, while the other smaller part became the French room. The Pet Club was moved from a site near the swimming pool to a more accessible place opposite the Art Room.

The School Plays in the Summer Term were major events. During the intervals a buffet supper was served with a bar selling wine and other drinks, and the evenings – there were three of them – were long and sociable. Before the arrival of Andrews, school plays had usually been put on in the Spring Term. His first production of 1979 set the theme for his subsequent ones. There was a performance of 'Papageno' from Mozart's Magic Flute, arranged by Bryan Gipps. After the supper interval the audience returned to the Ross Hall for Goldini's 'The Servant of Two Masters'. After this initial production there followed:-

1980	'The Pot of Gold' by Plautus, adapted by TMA
1981	'An Italian Straw Hat' by Labiche
1982	'The Liar' by Goldini (In May 'The Bride of Seville')
1983	'Gammer Gurton's Needle' by Mr S (In May 'Merlin's Brew', adapted from the Millard/Lawrence musical of 1972)
1984	'Farces Françaises'; the 37 Sous and the Spelling Mistakes by Labiche. (In the Spring term a musical by Hugh Mallarkey; 'Red Champagne')
1985	'Ralph Roister Doister' by Nicholas Udall (In the Spring term a musical by Hugh Mallarkey 'Tacitus')
1986	'Rudens' by Plautus
1987	'Le Médecin Malgré Lui' by Molière
1988	'Il Avaro Riformato – the Reformed Miser'
1989	'An Italian Straw Hat' by Labiche
1990	'The Liar' by Goldini
1991	'Rudens' by Plautus

As can be seen, Tim Andrews had a leaning towards Comedia dell'Arte which he adapted fairly freely, editing out the more tedious passages and sometimes introducing his own dialogue to speed the action or to bring in local references. These plays required and received a high standard of acting, and the organisation of the evenings promoted a feeling of 'occasion'.

There was, however, some comment about the type of play chosen and the lack of variety from year to year, as also about their suitability for young actors and partly young audiences. Tim Andrews' answer to this was '. . . if one wants to employ a good number of participants and produce a Festival atmosphere, then frivolous costume comedy is often the best choice'. Nevertheless, the hard work and enthusiasm which went into these plays left audiences feeling that they had enjoyed a real evening out.

1981 saw the arrival of John Hemmings from Eversley School in Southwold. Soon known to everyone as 'Jack', he was to make a great impression on the Junior School with his size, his beard and his stentorian voice. Beneath a gruff exterior he hid a genuine concern for his pupils and was eventually regarded by them with respect and even with affection. Mrs Pat Harrison came as Headmaster's Secretary in place of Mrs Nanette McLeish. She soon established the Office as the nerve centre of the school and her successes in breeding and showing Labradors were followed with much interest.

By mid-Summer advanced planning had been reached for new changing rooms to be sited in the area of the rosebeds on the West-facing side of the Cloisters. The plan was then to move the Library into the house from Wilson so as to occupy the space made available in the old changing rooms. The Wilson building would then be fitted out as a Games Room. A new flagpole was bought out of a gift from the parents of Mark Skingley and placed in the garden between Dining Room and the main road.

At the end of the Autumn Term Christopher Fitzgerald produced the first of his Extravaganzas, 'an evening of entertainment by the boys for the boys'. The Extravaganzas were in-house productions, a mixture of music hall and pantomime, planned but informal, with some Staff participation, but overall as a reason for the boys to let down their hair at the end of a long term before the more formal Christmas Feast.

Next year, 1982, saw the end of Andrew's House as a boarding annexe for the Junior School. At the end of the Summer Term it closed. The boys who had lodged there were absorbed into the dormitories in the main building, and Miss Betty Tozer was able to complete her retirement.

Ten years after he retired Harold Waters died. As Derek Ross wrote at the time, 'Harold was the special Mr Chips of the Junior School ...

5 J R 'Bob' Tozer, staff 1972–84.

6 D J Slater, staff 1972–87.

47 J T Packett, staff 1964–87.

48 The Choir outside the *Dom* at Aachen, Autumn 1987.

49 Mike and Jennifer Pomphrey.

50 Wilson being demolished, October 1993.

51 C J
FitzGerald,
1991.

52 Mike and Joanna Higham with Elizabeth, Rebecca and Pippa, July 1994.

53 Opening of the new wing by Mr D W R Evans, Autumn 1994.

so many old boys' lives have been the richer for knowing him'. The Strawberry Tea provision in his Will aroused wide media comment, and a four-minute slot was shown the next year on Anglia Television with the boys enjoying the fruits of his generosity.

The first stage of Tim Andrews' Development Scheme, the glazing of the Cloisters, was now complete. The Library was temporarily housed in the AV Room, the Games Room in Wilson was functioning and solar panels and new changing rooms in the Pavilion were installed. At Speech Day he was able to announce further progress in connection with the new changing rooms and also with an enlarged entrance hall. The latter was made possible by the Friends of Felsted to whose funds Harold Waters had made a substantial donation in his Will. The Friends also provided the means for furnishing and decorating the new Library.

In 1983, after five years of activity and planning, the development scheme initiated by Tim Andrews was completed. The changing rooms over the old Cloister rosebeds were in full use. The new Library with its beechwood shelves, carpeting and armchairs was a haven of peace, and the former 'Babes' changing room next door was turned into a Computer room with five machines linked to a disc drive unit. As more computers were acquired and more space needed as a result , the Computers were moved to the Central room of the junior classroom block, and the first Staff workroom set up in its place.

The original long passage leading to the Ross Hall was given a suspended ceiling with carpet tiles and spotlights. This was the passage where Harold Waters had displayed his Athletics and Rugger charts and down which the boys had slid over the quarry tiles on their way to meals.

The front hall was now refurbished, the Old Common Room, used by Miss Tozer as the stationery room, disappeared, and a Staff changing room and set of cloakrooms were made available at the back of the Ross Hall. A further spin-off was a library for paperback books, magazines and newspapers at the far end of the Cloisters in what had been used as the AV Room.

In January Christopher Fitzgerald left for a year's exchange with Allan Talbot from the Prep School of the Collegiate School of St Peter in Adelaide. In April Malcom Knowles arrived to take over Art from Val

Chater, and on a hot day in July, Dawn Foster married Simon Tibbitts (OF). She was to stay on at the Junior School for another two years before leaving to start a family. Hugh Mallarkey, who provided the two Spring term musicals, 'Red Champagne' and 'Tacitus' came in September. These highly enjoyable productions were written, composed and produced entirely by himself.

During the year a recording of the previous year's Sports Day was screened on television. It had been filmed by Channel 4 and, to quote a report, 'it was skilfully edited and had lots of humour as well as some marvellous action shots'.

From the beginning of 1984 the Junior School changed its name to 'Felsted Preparatory School', its fourth change of name, thus confirming at last its own identity with its own Headmaster, while remaining under the Governing Body of Felsted School.

Christopher Fitzgerald returned from a very successful stay in Australia, and Allan Talbot went back to Adelaide, after becoming engaged to Sheila Thompson, Senior Matron at the Prep. The success of this exchange prompted Michael and Joanna Higham to do the same – but this time for two years – from January 1985. In their place came David and Helen Toppin from Armidale School, New South Wales. On his return Michael Higham was appointed Senior Master following John Packett's retirement.

The previous year's developments were proving their worth; the main staircase was carpeted, and in the Ross Hall the stage lighting was overhauled with winch and pulley operated lighting bars.

J R Tozer (no relation of BT) left at the end of the Summer term, after teaching Mathematics for 13 years at the Prep in succession to Harold Waters. A career Gunner, Bob Tozer had commanded a Regiment before coming to Felsted. He coached happy and successful cricket XIs and was a fine cricketer himself. With his calm and cheerful approach to life he fitted well into the Prep School environment after the more rigorous disciplines of the Army.

Mrs Gill Wyatt also left after 7 years spent with the junior forms. Her previous experience had been gained with the British Colonial Service in Africa where she had been Headmistress of a Church school in the Sudan. Mrs Kate Edmond was to replace her. With two sons at the school, she quickly became absorbed into life at the Prep., and in 1992 was appointed Teacher In Charge of the newly established Pre-Prep.

After six eventful years Bryan Gipps left to become Head of Music at St Benedict's Ealing. As with his predecessors, he was a member of the Music Department and officially on the Senior School staff, and most of his time and attention was given to 'the other side of the road'. Nevertheless, he was able to maintain the high reputation of the Prep School Choir, and the list of Cathedrals at which they sang is impressive:

1978	November	St Edmondsbury
1979	February	Norwich
1980	April	Canterbury
	October	St Albans
1981	April	Chichester
1982	April	Salisbury, Wimbourne Minster, Bristol
1983	April	Canterbury
1984	April	Ripon
	May	Peterborough

His place was taken by Andrew Lowen. He was the Prep School's first Director of Music.

At Speech Day 1984 Andrews spoke of the growing demand for entry at 11 years. It was a portent of a change that was to happen in a short time on a larger scale. Those boys who passed an entrance test at 11 years were to gain automatic entrance to the Senior School without having to pass Common Entrance. Common Entrance results were to be used as a guide to setting in the Senior School. It was also realised that having to wear corduroy shorts after leaving their Primary School might act as a deterrent to many 11 year olds. For the first time, boys in the 4th Form and above were to wear long grey trousers.

During the wet Summer of 1985 the old paving stones outside the Cloisters, known as the 'Downs', the gift of parents of that name, were removed. They were replaced by a brick 'piazza' which took several months to lay owing to the precise levelling required and the constant bad weather. After thirty years of service the Scout Hut, which had been put up by Geoffrey Jameson and his Troop, had come to the end of its useful life. It was taken down and the space made available by its removal was given over to the boys for their gardens.

The sudden death of Mr Thomas Hunnable while on holiday in Scotland came as a sad shock. As a Governor for five years and as a parent and benefactor he was closely involved, together with his wife Edna, in all the activities of the Prep School, and his friendliness and spontaneous acts of generosity were much appreciated.

Hugh Mullarkey of 'Red Champagne' and 'Tacitus' fame left as did Malcom Knowles who went to a singing post at York Minster. Tristan Searle took over Mathematics from Bob Tozer, and, later as Director of Studies, became responsible for modernising the boys records, and in formalising subject syllabuses in connection with the introduction of the National Curriculum. Andrew Widdowson gave up most of his Senior School teaching to devote more of his time to the expanding field of Computer Studies at the Prep.

The view to the end of Cloisterfield was dramatically changed by the laying of a 'Hard Play' area on what had been the old Game 5 Rugger pitch. It has become an invaluable wet weather sports facility and is used as well for tennis and netball. Floodlighting was added later, providing a most useful recreation area during the winter evenings.

1986 and the years following were ones of consolidation after the many and varied improvements of the previous years. The first Leavers' Camp had taken place near Yarmouth in 1985, immediately after the Common Entrance Exams. The Camp was intended to fill in the time constructively between the end of the exams, and the announcement of the results. Activities included village surveys, drawing, bird watching, beach games and visits to local places of interest. Follow-up work back at school was combined with groups of leavers going off on Industry Days to six different places representing service industries and manufacturers. This first Leavers' Camp was such a success that it has been repeated every year since.

The departures of J T Packett and D J Slater in 1987 were the two major staff changes in 1987. John Packett came to Felsted in 1964. Although he had read History at Pembroke College, Oxford, he found himself in charge of Common Entrance and Scholarship French. On Harold Water's retirement he became Senior Master, and his wide knowledge of the Prep school world, his shrewd assessment of day to day problems and his penetrating comments on boys capabilities and characters proved invaluable.

David Slater taught Classics for 25 years at the Prep before moving on to King's School, Bruton in Somerset. As a teacher he combined the precision of a Classicist with a wry humour which could be seen in his meticulous and sometimes very critical reviews of School Plays. He also coached the Hockey XI with great success; his sides were seldom beaten and never outclassed. In Chapel he played the Organ and in Cathedrals all over the country he played for the Chapel Choir on its visits. He was self taught as an organist, and also played piano and harpischord either as a soloist or accompanist.

The 16th October 1987 was marked by the Great Storm which hit Southern and Eastern England. It was a week before electricity was restored but fortunately half term started next day and school routine was not disturbed. After breakfast the boys were kept indoors, as there was still a danger of falling branches and dislodged roof tiles. The largest tree to be blown down at the Prep was the False Acacia at the end of the Crittall block of classrooms, and little other damage was suffered.

During the year 1987/88 the Chapel Choir enjoyed, in Andrew Lowen's words 'one of the busiest and most exciting years in its life, and certainly the best since I have been here'. It included their first ever full length foreign tour, arranged by Professor Johannes Erger, whose hobby it had been to set up tours for the Aachen Cathedral Choir. In May 1987 this Choir had come to Felsted, and the reciprocal visit was made by the Prep School during the Autumn half term.

The first stop was in Aachen itself where the Choir sang the Ordinary of the Mass at High Mass in the Cathedral, the first Anglican Choir to do so. Concerts followed at Dulken, Breyell and Engelskirchen with a stopover at Cologne.

> The mountain scenery and fresh air of Engelskirchen made it a delightful stop. The mayoral reception and the hosts who entertained us will be long remembered. Not least the Graf von Spee who hosted a number of the 'gentlemen' in his castle and fed them on wild boar. The final concert was at Schweich on the Mosel where nearly all our hosts had a stake in a vineyard and were determined that we should try all the recent vintages. . . . I seem to

recall reaching my bed around three in the morning, although I can't
be certain . . . we sang parts of the Byrd Mass again, but suffered a
little from excess of a very local kind which effected some parts more
than others (Tenors again!) and led to some gross singing at times.

During a three day tour in the Easter 1988 holidays the Choir sang at
Bury St Edmunds and at Ely and gave a performance of Bach's Passion
at Thaxted as part of the Thaxted Festival. Towards the end of the
holidays they sang Evensong at St Paul's Cathedral, and two days later
took the place of Winchester's Cathedral Choir (on tour in America) at
the wedding of Jeremy Prior OF, son of Lord Prior, the former Cabinet
Minister. As well as the German tour and the Cathedral visits, during
the Summer term there were three Choral Evensongs and the annual
concert which included Constant Lambert's 'Rio Grande' and Poulenc's
'Gloria'. A truly vintage year for the Choir!

Andrew Lowen left in July 1990, after six years at the Prep, to become
Music Director of Kent College, Canterbury. As the first Director of
Music at the Prep he had had to fashion a job which had not really
existed before. Appreciating that the Chapel Choir was the flagship
of the school's music, he did everything possible, with Tim Andrews'
enthusiastic encouragement, to further the Choir's reputation.

At the end of the Summer term 1991 Tim and Chrissi Andrews left
Felsted to take over Downside School, Purley. Andrews had accom-
plished much in improving the facilities of the school, and his efforts
had done much to delay the trend away from boarding. His personal
interest in the Choir and his ambitious productions of the School Plays
were two of the many ways in which he successfully promoted the school,
and he and Chrissi created a happy atmosphere which was plain for
visitors to see.

8

M P Pomphrey 1992 –

In January 1992 Michael and Jennifer Pomphrey left Gepp's House, Felsted Senior School, to take over the Prep. Although without previous direct experience of running a junior school, Michael Pomphrey knew much already about the Prep, as his son Stephen had been a pupil there and his work for the Friends of Felsted had involved him in many of the development projects. During the Autumn term interregnum Michael Higham had assumed the duties of Headmaster, and successfully ensured that the routines of school life were continued normally.

Two fundamental decisions were taken by the Governors in early 1992. The first was that there should be full co-education in both the Prep and Senior Schools, the Prep to start in September 1993.

The second was the establishment of a Pre Prep for boys and girls from 4-8 years starting in the Autumn. These decisions altered the character of the Prep School dramatically. The decline in boarding had already had its effect; the changes announced in 1992 meant that the old style, 8-13 year old, boys only school was to conform with the social and economic demands of the late '80s and '90s. However radical the change was to be, there was a universal determination from everyone involved to keep the same characteristics which had marked the school, its warm and friendly atmosphere and its commitment to high achievement in the classroom and on the games field.

During the Spring and Summer of 1992 the four classroom block next to the Ranger's Patch was converted to Pre-Prep use and an additional classroom built to accommodate the expected rise in numbers. The Pre-Prep opened in the Autumn term with 43 pupils. In charge was Mrs Kate Edmond who had already spent eight years teaching in the Prep and had taken a leading part in planning the new department, overseeing the classrooms' layout and the play areas. These were set up in what had originally been the Scout Patch. The whole Pre Prep area was fenced off and placed out of bounds to the rest of the school.

That same Autumn term saw the arrival of the first girls at the Prep School since Anne and Mary Telfer at Canon ffrome during the war. These 'pioneers' were Elizabeth and Rebecca Higham, Sarah and Sophie Harrington and Rebecca Benfield. As separate facilities were not yet ready for them, they had to make use of the Headmaster's House. Soon major alterations were being made in the main building to provide girls only areas for September 1993. Cromwell passage was sealed off, the dormitories in it refurnished and the old Resident Master's flat given over to a living in Matron. Downstairs, the Library and Staff workroom (in the pre-Andrews changing rooms) were equipped for use as girls' changing rooms. The Library now made yet another of its many moves into the Cloister dayrooms. The senior boys' dayroom became an enlarged Staff workroom with access to the School Office.

Autumn term 1993 opened with everything in place for welcoming the girls to the Prep. Within a short time the 'petticoat invasion' had been accepted by the large majority of the boys, and the new girls soon became absorbed into the life of the school.

The figures below for Autumn 1993 show how far the composition of the School had changed recently.

Prep.	Day	107	Boys	95
	Boarding	33	Girls	45
	Total 140			
Pre-Prep.	78 – a slight predominance of boys over girls			

Pressure on space was now acute. Four classrooms had been taken over by the Pre Pre with the prospect of numbers there increasing still further. The dayrooms had been surrendered to the Library and Staff workroom. Out of commission dormitories and other rooms in the main house were used as temporary dayrooms, but the lack of space was still felt, especially in the winter months. A plan was therefore approved to build a 2 storey extension to the Cloister wing. The first phase of the building was to include four classrooms, the second phase would go forward when practicable. And so, in October 1993 the Wilson building, put up in 1947, which had played so many different roles, was knocked down, and work started on the foundations for the new classrooms.

After thirteen years at the Prep Christopher Fitzgerald left in July 1991 to become Under Master at Chigwell Junior School. On John Packett's departure he became the first Senior Resident master in charge of the boarders, and developed many aspects of the post which would be followed by his successors. As Head of English he started the Debate Club and the Poetry Competition, and the exuberant side of his personality found expression in his Christmas Extravaganzas. His position 'upstairs' was taken over by Mark and Jackie Weldon for whom the redundant Canon ffrome and Morris dormitories were converted into a flat.

In July 1992 Ian Roberts left after five years as Head of French and enthusiastic Choir member. He introduced the use of computers in teaching the language, and initiated a series of frequent visits and exchanges to France. These visits were continued by his replacement, Miss Gill Brown – who also introduced the popular activity of horse-riding to the school for the first time.

In March 1992 Felsted was saddened to learn of the death of Rev Derek Ross just a year after he and Enid had celebrated their Golden Wedding. It was twenty one years since he had retired from the Junior School as it then was, but the memory of what he had achieved was still very much alive.

Another death, which much affected his colleagues, was that of John Hemmings, always known as 'Jack', who had been Head of Geography from 1981 until he was obliged to go on sick leave because of recurring cancer. A man of imposing bulk before his illness, bearded, and with a gruff and aggressive exterior, he was nonetheless a most effective teacher who earned the respect and even the affection of his pupils.

In July 1994 Mike Higham left Felsted after 19 years as Head of Science and, latterly, as Deputy Headmaster, in order to take up the

Headmastership of Moulsford Preparatory School. A talented sports-man himself, he coached the 1st Rugger XV through many successful seasons.

At the start of Autumn Term 1994 the new classroom wing was opened by Mr David Evans and appropriately named after him. As former Chairman of Governors he had always shown close interest in the fortunes of the Prep. The Evans wing was the first substantial addition to the school buildings since the Ross Hall was put up in 1971.

Appendix 1

F. Jacob, Esq.

Mr Jacob sailed for India on Sept 7 – not on a pleasure tour but to start a career. He intends to work under Mr Tyndale-Biscoe at Srinagar, teaching in the C.M.S. School. His hours are to be 10 to 3: he hopes to play a round of golf daily and to swim the lake; some will remember the number of miles across it. Not many men go out East for the first time when over sixty, and fewer still to restart work. But Mr Jacob is exceptional, exceptional in his courage, in his physique, in his ideals, and in his practice of them. Some forty years ago he was an outstanding undergrad at Cambridge; he was an International Rugger Blue; he played water polo for the Varsity; he rowed in the Caius boat; played in the Caius Cricket XI; ran in their athletic team, and was a member of the Corps. He took the Mathematical Tripos and then the Modern Language; he studied at Paris and Göttingen, and gained the Diplôme de la Guilde Internationale. Two years' work at Bradfield and seven years at Cheltenham preceded his marriage. In 1907 he accepted a very pressing invitation to take charge of our Junior House. The fortunes of the House were then at a low ebb; the tide slowly turned, and then came sure, merited and unbroken success. His system of training was a strenuous one; the youngest was encouraged to imitate the most efficient and to endeavour to surpass him; he was encouraged by instruction, help, sympathy and reward. But the reward lay not in prizes but in honour, and especially the honour of a group, called a League, or of the House. Many trophies were offered for competition, chief among them a massive silver trophy, which Mr Jacob provided for moral efficiency. The system, which was based on self-discipline and self-development, abolished the perpetual supervision by masters, but put an enormous burden of detail and sympathy upon them. Yet Mr Jacob found time – he rose at 6 – to put his many parts at the service of the main School. The change from 'Soccer' to 'Rugger' would have been long delayed had he not been available to coach. In the war, when rejected for active service, he took a commission in our OTC. He has made time year after year to judge our Gymnastic Competition, officiate at the Boxing, and judge our swimming. His many gifts were devoted to the welfare of Felsted; he lived to serve. Shattering bereavement intensified his purpose, and he gave his service without reserve, cheerfully, without looking back, and with a single eye. May he win in Kashmir the admiration, affection and gratitude that came to him as his due at Felsted.

The FELSTEDIAN Dec. 1933

Appendix 2

The Prep. Thirty Years Ago

In some respects my memories of the Prep. and my first years there are as vivid as yesterday, in others, time and experiences in Mid. and Far East have expunged the impressions or blurred the details in my mind.

F.J. (Fred Jacob) remains a Goliath figure. In his navy blue blazer, grey flannel trousers and cloth cap he still stalks with steady gait, pausing to flick out his silver retractable pencil and after slowly scratching his ear with it to make notes on his celluloid note book – probably 'Points off' for somebody who had his shoe laces undone, or had committed some other misdemeanour.

Jacob had a great reputation for perfect self-control. In his England rugger days in the scrum it was said he had never been roused even to the point of saying damn. This imperturbability remained, he never appeared to be more than slightly angry, never raised his voice, and always spoke in a slow judicial tone worthy of the Lord Chancellor delivering a solemn judgment. Only once did I remember a laugh destroy this composure, and that at my expense. In the middle of Psalm reading by J. at evening prayers, when the Psalm referred to flowing waters, this solemn moment was enriched by sounds illustrative of the Psalm and I was hastily removed in tears with wet trousers to the matron. J. was unable to finish the Psalm. Whether through kindness of heart, or the fact that this record of control was broken I do not know, but no punishment ensued and the incident was allowed to be forgotten.

Apart form Jacob there was the Duck or Matron Haley, bespectacled and hiding behind a leather face a kind heart. She looked after our ailments, doled out pills, ladled grease on our chapped legs in winter and took our temps. In mellow mood she would tell us tales of her internment in Germany in 1914–18 where she had been before then a children's governess.

Next to her room on the first floor was Tommy's. Tommy Tomlinson and Duck were oil and water, or cat and dog, and many a feudal duel between the two would cheer us up and hasten the end of term. Tommy with a face remarkably like a monkey with shiny pate and little hair was mad keen on hockey and much kinder than his appearance. The hockey eleven should have fond memories of his end of term 'Gut.' It was a real beanfeast at what is now Bootes Cafe. At half time we used to run round and round the table to make room for more.

Tommy and Duck took turns at doing our weekly bath. Almost invariably the water was too hot to get into in the winter and we shivered on the edge sometimes gazing at the 'Cleanliness is next to Godliness' in illuminated letters on the mantlepiece. I have never looked to see if this text is still there.

I was in Cromwell dorm. It was the safest as it was at the end of the passage, and if our scouts were good we got fair warning of the slosh of slippers as Tommy crept along the passage to catch us out. A Booby trap of house shoes balanced on the top of a door ajar worked too well one night and cracked down on his bald head, when he raided us and earned for us an immediate whacking.

China wash basins, jugs and 'Tolly Mugs' on a bench down the middle of the dorm, were standard equipment. One winter we had was so cold that we were actually able to lay a slide down the dorm. At the head of the dorm, was a small boxroom useful for midnight feasts.

The day started with cold showers and six leg ups and press ups. We were always hungry and sometimes a banana would be the main course for breakfast.

The League and points system worked rather as I think it does today, only very much more so, and the number of points won or lost could be measured in hundreds. Occasionally one had to write out twenty lines in copper plate handwriting such as. Don't be a human slug (if anyone was caught leaving an untidy mess around). Others were – Place your hand before your mouth before you yawn because no one wants to see the inside of it. Or, Don't blow your nose like a plough boy.

Towards the middle of my prep. days Follyfield started and we began to play Rugger on it. In addition to a large number of stones there was also an unpleasant number of cinders that had been lain on the field, and tackling often incurred most unpleasant gashes on the knees. We had a 'Collaring Cup' to compete for each year and when we moved on to this field it needed real to determination to keep up one's tackling standards. The stones were dealt with by J. and us. He spent hours clearing the field from stones and we could earn points for picking up stones. I think the scale was one point for 25 stones and I know there was some real slave-driving by keen league captains. Also we could thus build up a reserve to counteract any projected crimes which would lose us points. The results of our labours are shewn in the playing field today.

Before Follyfield we used to trek down to a field below the Bury. The route took us by Prysties along the back of the San, and across a field or two to the ground. On our way we passed a potato clamp which usually had a few potatoes lying about. These came home with us and roasting took place in the Tool shed with 'Boykies' connivance. He was J's gardner. Sometimes we used the stoves in the Gym but these were dangerous as the smell gave us away. In our hunger we enjoyed chestnuts and apples obtained from Scriveners. Also sugar beet cut into strips and sucked was most satisfying but too much had most violent aperient results. 'On the Bill' we could get toothpaste. At that time one could get a new brand known as 'Newmix.' This had a fruit centre, with cream filling, and it was not unknown for a tube to be consumed in one night.

Another character who taught us was T.C. He put the wind up me and probably many others. I was on first acquaintance convinced that he was a madman and he certainly did his best to create that impression. His arrival from the Senior School was a triumphant dramatic entry. Stalking in, nose in air, and sometimes holding aloft a banana. He was capable of anything. He would prance up and down the room like a caged tiger. In his milder moments he was great fun and his laughter resounded throughout the school, as also did his screams of fury when aroused. The dunce would be made to climb up into the window and recite 'Little birds of the air, help me to solve this sum.' In his violent moments he was noted for his sandwiches which were prepared by bringing both hands violently together, the filling being the victim's face and ears.

Tremlett Wills or Trembling Willy, as we knew him, was the School Doctor. He was reputed to have served as a bonesetter in the days of sailing ships, and he was a great character with a long grey beard and a cheerful chuckling laugh. He seemed especially amused when slicing styes on eyes which he did with a long fine knife.

Every day, winter and summer, we went to the baths. On certain days Mr. Ebert taught us to swim. Boxing and gym were under his capable supervision and it is nice to see him still going strong. During the winter we got ghastly chaps on our knees coming from the baths. In the evening these were dealt with by the Duck, who ladled grease on them from a large jar. Apart from this, swimming kept us very fit on top of everything else.

We had tough and happy times in those days, but if I had to choose between then and now, I would not hesitate to choose the modern.

P J B CHURCH
(JH 1925-1929)
From Y.F. Autumn 1954.

Peter Church had two sons at the Junior House, William from 1950 and David from 1959. He was a good friend of the School and became Clerk to the Governors of Felsted. He died in 1991.

Appendix 3

The Origin of Our League Names

Both boys and parents often ask how our Leagues got their names, and we give below short notes concerning the five personages represented which we hope will be of interest.

LORD RICHE

Richard, Lord Riche, was the founder of the School. Born about 1480 he was the son of a wealthy London mercer and became a lawyer. He was appointed Solicitor-General to King Henry VIII and later became Speaker of the Commons and President of the Court of Augmentations, the commission appointed to carry out the Dissolution of the Monasteries. For his services he was rewarded with the grant of something like a hundred manors, including Leez Priory. From 1547-52 he held the Great Seal. No doubt that the monks had abused their trust and there was reason for closing the monasteries, but Lord Riche could not forget that their help must certainly be missed in the parishes which had enjoyed it. Especially would the boys miss the education that used to be given at the monasteries. With such thoughts he ordered the first deed of the Felsted Foundation to be prepared, which was to include a chantry, almshouses, a gift of herrings during Lent, and a School. The School foundation deed is dated May 21st 1564. In it Lord Riche lays down that the school is to be a Grammar School, that is, a school in which Latin is taught and that the number of boys was to be 80. He gave detailed instructions for the yearly school service in Felsted Church. Its day, hour and form were laid down by him, even the very words of the Collect. He also gave us our coat-of-arms and the motto 'Garde ta Foy'.

CROMWELL

Oliver Cromwell was himself a native of Huntingdonshire but his relation with Felsted School was very close. His wife was the daughter of Sir James Bourchier who owned Grandcourts and at Cambridge he was acquainted with Martin Holbeach, the famous Felsted Headmaster of Puritan times. He sent his four boys to the School. Robert died while still at school at the age of 18, his next brother Oliver served as a Cornet of Horse in the Civil War and came to a mysterious end in 1644. Richard was therefore left as his father's heir and was the only one of Cromwell's heirs who seemed to inherit no spark of his father's genius. Perhaps it was his knowledge of the young man's weaknesses that made Cromwell unwilling to have the Protectorship made hereditary. Richard was Protector after his father for a short while, and Felsted can therefore claim to be the only public school to have educated a ruler of this country.

Of other, and better stuff, was Henry, Cromwell's fourth son. He became Major-General of the Forces in Ireland which he administered with a firm hand. The name of Cromwell League commemorates the School's connection with the whole family.

GASELEE

General Sir Alfred Gaselee was at Felsted from 1853 to 1861. At school he showed great promise and was both a Prefect and a Cricket colour. Immediately after leaving school he was granted a commission in the Indian Army and saw service on the North West Frontier, winning his first decoration before he was twenty. For forty years he was on almost continuous service in India, Abyssinia, Africa and China, where his energetic counsels and skilful guidance were largely instrumental in relieving Peking during the Boxer riots of 1900. He was a Governor of the School from 1910 until his death in 1918 and showed especial interest in the Junior House. He laid the foundation stone of the old Grignon Hall.

SMYTHIES

Charles Alan Smythies was a courageous and great-hearted missionary, a born statesman as well as a deeply religious and entirely fearless Bishop. He was at Felsted at the same time as Gaselee and during Mr Grignon's Headmastership. He became curate and then vicar of Roath, the rapidly growing suburb and port of Cardiff. His straight talks and conspicuous manliness attracted the dockers and workmen who were willing to give up part of their precious dinner hours to listen to him. in 1883 he was consecrated Bishop for Central Africa, a diocese of some 3,000 square miles, and later Bishop of Zanzibar. His cathedral was built on the site of the last slave market of the world.

Africa had only been opened up by David Livingstone some 20 years before, the slave traffic had been suppressed but 10 years and none of the native languages had been reduced to writing. In spite of these difficulties and the opposition of the German colonists, Smythies set about his great work of the selection and training of natives as evangelists to their own people. This work meant constant travelling, always on foot, mostly through forests, often waist-deep in mud, and after walking 2,000 miles a year for 5 years the Bishop decided that the diocese was too big for one man. He founded Nyasa as a separate bishopric, but he had already worn himself out in spite of his wonderful physique: few men could equal his powers of endurance. He died at sea on his way home to England on May 7th 1894.

GRIGNON

The Rev W S Grignon, MA, was Headmaster of Felsted from 1856 to 1875 and has been called the 'second founder' of the School. When Mr Grignon came, all the boys and masters lived in the Old School House (now Ingram's Close) and all teaching was still carried out in the Old School by the Church. Under Mr Grignon the School prospered and soon outgrew the old buildings and the old playground. It was determined to build anew and by degrees the present school block rose on the new site. In the Church the gallery was no longer able to hold the school, who overflowed into the chancel, and mainly through Mr Grignon's efforts the school chapel was opened on Founder's Day 1873.

In 1861 Mr Grignon founded and commanded the Rifle Volunteers, one of the earliest school corps. The Grignon Hall is named in his memory, and his portrait is in the central panel on the platform.

Reproduced from the Junior House Magazine of Spring Term 1939.

Appendix 4

Assistant Staff at the Preparatory School from 1920

W A Tomlinson	1911-32
H R St. A Davies	1916-32
A H Andrew	1932-34 (HM Felsted 1943-47)
A U Payne	1932-34 (then Felsted)
C J Fletcher	1934-39
P L Sherwood	1934–36
F E F Doubleday	1934-37
Rev P M Osborn	1934-39
O I Simpson	1936-45 (then Felsted)
M C G Hooton	1936-45 (then Felsted)
R N Towers	1937-41
Rev L R Buttle	1940-41
Miss M M Fielding	1940-42
Maj C P Sparrow (OF)	1941-46
R J van Leuvan (OF)	1941-46
Mrs J R Sprott	1942-50
Rev A J Taylor	1945-46
H G Waters (OF)	1946-72
Rev G K Booth	1946-47

J H C Walker	1946-51
C R Tunks (OF)	1946-47
E W I Mason (OF)	1947-50
G S Jameson	1947-59
J H R Churchill	1947-51
Miss R W Spiller	1948-51
J C Harrowing	1948-49
C K Hills	1949-53
N W P Davies	1951-54
R E Ferris	1951-53
A H Birchall	1959-64
Miss B Tozer	1950-79
Miss J M Reynolds	1953-55
P J Murphy	1953-55
G B Stanley	1953-59
G W Bullard	1954-60
T H Steed	1955-59
D J Parry	1955-57
Maj J H Benoy (OF)	1957-63
Miss S M Johnson	1957
T J Bale	1957-58
Miss J Maxwell	1958-59
M W Kelham	1959-63
D S Rymer	1959-60
H Eden	1960-65
W H Carr	1960-61
Miss R Trew	1960-66
P F Higgins	1961-78
M R Griffin	1961-66
J T Packett	1964-87
M F Edwards	1964-65
M R Smith (OF)	1958-61 (and Felsted)
A J Bailey	1965-69
D J Armour	1965-95
H R Watts	1966-79
Miss P Mallinson	1967

P D R Millard	1967-72
Miss E M Bennett	1968-69
B Lippett	1969-75
Miss G H Cresswell	1970-77
Miss C Coughtrey	1971-74
JR Tozer	1972-84
D J Slater	1972-87
M J Walsh	1974-76
Mrs M Ballingall	1975-76
M J Higham	1975-94
Mrs D J Barsby	1976-77
G J Garrett	1976-83
Mrs M G Wyatt	1977-84
Miss G F J Williams	1977-78
C J FitzGerald	1978-91
Mrs V J Chater (OF)	1978-82
Miss D K Foster	1978-85
R A G Cox	1979-81
J K Hemmings	1981-91
A Talbot	1983/4 and 1989-
J M Knowles	1983-85
H E Mullarkey	1983-85
A J Lowen	1984-90
Mrs C M Edmond	1984-
T J Searle	1985-
D M Toppin	1985-87
Mrs C J Jessop	1985-91
Miss C A Hall	1986-
R A Fowke	1987-90
I S Roberts	1987-92
T K A Robertson	1987-
B M R Lawson	1987-90
R A Muttitt	1990-94
M C Parkinson	1991-92
Mrs J M Clayman	1991-
M D Weldon	1991-

T K W Eager	1991-
A H J Spooner	1991-
Miss G M Brown	1992-
T W P Hills	1993-
C H N Poyntz	1994-
Miss A A Groucutt	1994-

Pre-Preparatory

i.c. Mrs C M Edmond	1984-
Mrs C Muttitt	1992-94
Mrs L A Jagger	1992-
Mrs S Randall	1992-
Mrs E J Pockley	1993-
Mrs L J Lane	1994-
Mrs S L Goodfellow	1994-

Source: Alumni Felstedienses – with additions.

Appendix 5

Names

During its one hundred years the preparatory part of Felsted School has been given four different names, reflecting its changing status. They are:

1895-1903	The Preparatory House
1903-1956	The Junior House
1956-1983	The Junior School
1983-	Felsted Preparatory School

Index

Addis, R, 47–8
Alexandra, Princess, 49
Andrew, AH, 31, 37, 39
Andrew pavilion, 39, 40, 62
Andrew's House, 39, 70
Andrews, TM, 67–76
Art Room, 55

Backhouse, Rev JH, 2
Barsby, RJ, 63–4, 67
Bickersteth, Rev J, 27, 29, 32, 34
Birchall, AH, 54, 55-6
Briggs, Prof. R, 56
Bullard, GW, 41
Burleigh brothers, 47
Byford, Mrs O, 68

Canon ffrome Court, 32–5
Cattrall, RL, 56
Cecil, Mrs, 22, 24
Cecil, R, 24
Chandler, P, 50
Chater, Mrs V, 67, 71
Church, PJB, 83–6
Church, SM, 63
Churchill, JHR, 38, 40
Cloister wing, 27–8

Co-education, 77–8
Cooper, T, 25, 85–6
Cresswell, Miss GH, 63, 67
Crittall, JF, 23
Cromwell, Oliver, 88

Dalton, Rev HA, 1, 8
Davies, HR St A, 17, 25
Drake, Commander & Mrs, 53
Duckworth, LG, 2

Ebert, Sgt., 17, 25, 34, 86
Eden, W, 53
Edmond, Mrs CM, 72–3, 78
Eldred, M, 63
Elwyn's House, 7, 36
Evans wing, 79, 80

Felgate, PS, 47
FitzGerald, CJ, 67, 70–2, 79
Follyfield, 24
Ford, Rev LSK, 39
Foster, TR, 53
Foster-Tibbitts, Mrs D, 67, 72
Frith, Mrs, 14, 16
Frith, Dr WS, 4, 8

Gaselee, Gen Sir A, 88
Gipps, BJ, 67, 69, 73
Grégoire, Rev AV, 4

Hamilton, JEB & TH, 13
Harrison, Mrs P, 70
Hemmings, JK, 70,79
Higgins, PF, 48–9, 50–2, 61, 65, 67
Higham MJ, 61, 68, 72, 77, 79, 80
Hobby House (CDT room), 32
Holmes, Sir M, 23
Hooton, MCG, 34, 38
Hopton, Mrs, 33, 35
Howard, JRE, 25
Hunnable, TF, 60, 62, 64, 74

Jacob, F, 9–26, 35, 81–3
Jameson, GS, 38, 40–3, 46, 48, 56, 73
Jones, Mrs M, 60

Kelham, MW, 56
Kendall, KGF, 52–3, 59
Key, A, 6–7
Knowles, JM, 74

Langton, FA, 63
Lippet, B, 61
Lowen, AJ, 73, 75–6
Lucking, MT, 48

Malleson, JHF, 29
Mason, EWI, 38
Millard, D, 45

Millard, Mrs M, 61
Miller, CM, 1–4, 15–16
Morgan, DH, 25
Morris, BS, 37–43, 62
Morris, S, 47
Mullarkey, HE, 72, 74

Neal, JR, 29
Nield, Miss J, 34

Oliver, RM, 56

Packett, JT, 60, 63, 68, 72, 74–5
Pemberton, OJB, 57–65
Pomphrey, MP, 77–80
Pre-Prep, 77–8

Raymond, A, 68
Reindorp, Bishop GE, 23
Reynolds, J, 47–8
Riche, Lord, 87–8
Ripton, Mr & Mrs J, 58
Roberts, IS, 79
Ronaldson, Mr & Mrs A, 53–4
Ross, Rev DL, 37, 45–56, 62, 79
Ross, Mrs E, 45–6
Ross Hall, 55
Rugger, introduced, 11

Scouting, 41–3, 48–9
Searle, TJ, 74
Shadbolt, PB, 63
Simpson, OI, 32, 34–5, 38
Slater, DJ, 68, 75
Smith, MR, 56

INDEX

Smythies, Bishop, 89
Sparrow, Maj. CP, 34
Stanley, GB, 56
Stephenson, brothers, 63–4
Stephenson, Dr F, 4, 9
Stephenson, Rev F, 8–9, 27
Swimming pool, 59

Talbot, A, 71–2
Telfer, Rev AC, 27–37, 62
Thorne, GH, 25, 34
Thorne, Mrs E, 22
Thorp, JWD, 2, 8
Tomlinson, WA, 17, 24–5, 84
Tozer, Miss B, 65, 67, 70
Tozer, JR, 61, 64, 68, 72, 74
Trafford, Mrs, 32
Trew, Miss R, 53, 55
Turner, KB, 13–15
Tyndale Biscoe, 26

Walker, HE, 16-25
Walker, JHC, 38, 43
Warwick, Earl & Countess of, 5
Waters, HG, 38, 40, 42–3, 47–8,
    57–9, 70–1
Watts, HR, 68
Watts, NWR, 63
Wilson building, 40–1, 79
Wyattt, Mrs MG, 68, 72

Yeldham, IJ, 63
Young Felstedian, 40

99